The Best of the Best

RICARDO

The Best of the Best

100 Recipes We (and You!) Love the Most

appetite

Library and Archives Canada Cataloguing in Publication is available upon request.
ISBN: 978-0-525-61248-3
eBook ISBN: 978-0-525-61249-0

Printed in China

The authorized representative in the EU for product safety and compliance is Penguin Random House Ireland, Morrison Chambers, 32 Nassau Street, Dublin D02 YH68, Ireland, https://eu-contact.penguin.ie

Published in Canada by Appetite by Random House®, a division of Penguin Random House Canada Limited.
320 Front Street West, Suite 1400
Toronto, Ontario, M5V 3B6, Canada
penguinrandomhouse.ca

10 9 8 7 6 5 4 3 2 1

appetite
by RANDOM HOUSE

Penguin Random House

RICARDO MEDIA
Chef and Author: Ricardo
Directors—Content and Creation: Maude Bourcier-Bouchard and Myriam Huzel (interim)
Studio Director—Creation and Production: Josée Berniqué
Art Director: Geneviève Larocque
Recipe Development: Lisa Birri, Nicolas Cadrin, Isabelle Deschamps Plante, Kareen Grondin, Alexane Labonté, Etienne Marquis and Laurence Viens
Recipe Tester: Danielle Bessette
Editor: Charline-Ève Pilon
Translation: Vicki Karigiannis and Michelle Diamond
Photographers: Sophie Carrière, Maude Chauvin, David De Stefano, Dana Dorobantu, Christian Lacroix, Mathieu Lévesque and Jean-Michel Poirier
Graphic Design: Ève Paquet and Etienne Derepentigny
Food Stylists: Nicolas Cadrin, Anne Gagné, Etienne Marquis and Nataly Simard
Accessories Stylists: Caroline Nault, Sylvain Riel and Caroline Simon
Photo Retouching: Jean-Michel Poirier
Graphic Artists: Karine Breton and Pascale Payant
Project Manager—Projects and Production: Martine Lauriault and Gaelle Mahouin
Recipe Revision: Louise Faucher
President: Brigitte Coutu
General Director: Mireille Arteau
Vice-President Communications and Marketing: Nathalie Carbonneau
Marketing Advisor: Audrey-Anne Guay

ricardocuisine.com

If a recipe marked FREEZES WELL does not already include specific freezing instructions, it can be frozen after cooking. Let cool completely and then transfer to a freezer bag or airtight container. Freeze up to 6 months.

Contents

Our 100 Best Recipes 9
How Did We Create the Best Recipes? 10
Appetizers & Sides 12
Breakfasts 46
Main Dishes 74
Desserts 156
Thank You to the Best Team 219
Index 220

Our 100 Best Recipes

Over the years, my test kitchen team and I have developed more than 9,000 recipes. From those thousands of recipes, we handpicked and perfected a select few to create a subcategory on our website, ricardocuisine.com, simply named "The Best." These recipes in particular have been huge hits among our readers and have become classics in many homes. And of those recipes, you will find the 100 best of the best in this book.

But what does it take to turn a good recipe into a "best" recipe? Is it adding hard-to-find ingredients or using fancy kitchen equipment? No. As a chef for over 25 years and host of my own cooking show, I can tell you that creating the best version of a recipe is about rolling up your sleeves and making it again and again (and again!)—tweaking an ingredient here, adjusting a technique there—all the while sampling every revision of the dish until it tastes like the very best version of itself you can imagine.

Yes, that sometimes means cooking the same dish seven times in a row, and almost always means making a few mistakes along the way. It has also meant frying and tasting and tweaking batch after batch of French fries (try 45 pounds of potatoes!) over the span of an entire week until the results were both perfectly crisp on the outside and perfectly warm and fluffy on the inside (see the recipe on p. 15).

The path of figuring out how to perfect our best recipes isn't one I traveled alone. Over the years, a talented group of test kitchen chefs have been beside me, developing recipes for our magazine, website and books. Many other colleagues have been there too, happy and willing taste-testers, abandoning their desks and dropping by the test kitchen to sample and vote for their favorite version of the recipe in development that day. I think back to that potato-filled week, and there were dozens of people crowded into the kitchen, turning it into a veritable French fry stand! It's moments like those—and many, many hours of hard work and dedication—that helped shape the recipes you'll find in the following pages.

As you flip through this book, be sure to read the explanation on each page for how exactly we achieved each best version of that recipe. You'll find our notes on, for example, the specific variety of an ingredient we found adds the most flavor, or the details on the precise cooking method we used to create the best texture. Read those notes and you'll see why these 100 recipes are the very best—the recipes that made it past our extensive trial and error phase to earn their place of pride in this book.

I want you to cook and bake each of these 100 recipes with confidence and pride. From our Barbecue Ribs (p. 143) to our Cheesecake (p. 203), these recipes are approachable, easy to make and foolproof. And if some seem a little more involved, I promise the result makes them well worth the effort.

I hope you find the same joy in the kitchen making them as my team and I did creating them.

How Did We Create the Best Recipes?

Well, the development process was certainly an adventure! Each recipe would begin with its selection, and we kept classic dishes at the heart of our approach. For a recipe to be a good candidate for a "best" version, it needs to speak to as many people as possible. We wanted the recipe to inspire discussion or debate on how to prepare it—and we'd know we were on to a good thing when there were lots of opinions!

We also gleaned inspiration from our own culinary experiences and memories; our conversations on new recipes that we wanted to take to the next level; and our commitment to existing dishes that we simply had to make the must-try version of.

We also paid particular attention to the advice of our online community. Some of the recipes you'll see here weren't deliberately developed as "best" versions but simply became that way over time because of how much our readers (you!) loved them. When we'd see a stream of glowing online reviews—as was the case with our Ultra-Moist Banana Bread (p. 59)—of course we listened!

RECIPE DEVELOPMENT

The best version of a recipe is, of course, subjective. Our best paella could be different from that of a Valencia-born Spaniard. The same goes for our best-ever spaghetti sauce when compared to your mother's recipe. So we began each recipe's development by researching and reading up on its history, finding out what's been done with it in the past, and cross-referencing that information with what our test kitchen team already knew about the ingredients or methods used. Then we'd call everything into question, interrogate the recipe and develop a few hypotheses to experiment with.

Once we had a general idea of the recipe, we'd focus on the ingredients list and preparation. We tested various cooking times, preparation methods and seasonings until we achieved our desired results. Then we'd test and test again, leaving nothing to chance and no stone unturned.

THE PERFECT BALANCE

The proposed best version of each recipe was then tasted by all members of the test kitchen and me, and we'd also invite feedback from everywhere else. At this stage, anything and everything was possible! The recipe was yet to be published, so we would adapt or change the recipe after a photoshoot, for example. We'd take all the feedback given and adapt and make further changes until the dish was perfect.

FINAL RECIPE

Our test kitchen was satisfied with a recipe only once it met the preferences and expectations of each person involved in the process. Only then would we agree that we'd made it the "best" we possibly could and place the metaphorical seal of approval on the recipe.

THE DEVELOPMENT OF OUR BEST CARROT CAKE ON PAGE 197 TOOK SEVERAL ATTEMPTS. HERE'S A GLIMPSE OF THE TRIALS WE DID.

1 For this attempt, we tested an imposing three-layer cake. We needed a very firm frosting that could sustain the weight of the layers, but it ended up too sweet for our taste.

2 We tried baking this one in a loaf pan, but it took too long and the cake started to caramelize along the edges, which we didn't enjoy.

3 We included raisins and nuts in this version baked in a square cake pan. The idea was a good one, but it ended up tasting more like a muffin than a cake.

4 Adding pineapple turned out to be a winning choice in this final version, which became our very best. We cut the sugar nearly in half, stacked two layers of cake and covered it in frosting for a very indulgent final result.

The Best Appetizers

Homemade Fries

PREPARATION 20 minutes
CHILLING 1 hour
COOKING 20 minutes
SERVINGS 4

5 to 6	large white potatoes, peeled or not
	Vegetable oil, for frying
6	slices bacon

Using a knife or French fry cutter, slice the potatoes into sticks about 1⁄2 inch (1 cm) thick.

In a large bowl of cold water, soak the potatoes for 30 minutes or up to 24 hours in the refrigerator. Drain and pat very dry with a clean kitchen towel.

Preheat the oil in a deep fryer to 300°F (150°C). Line a baking sheet with paper towels.

Place the bacon slices in the hot oil around the fryer basket. Blanch half of the potatoes at a time in the oil for 8 minutes. Watch out for splattering. Drain on the baking sheet. Let cool. Refrigerate for 30 minutes or until the potatoes are cold. Remove the bacon slices and set them aside for another use.

Increase the temperature of the fryer to 350°F (180°C). Line another baking sheet with paper towels. Preheat the oven to 200°F (95°C).

Fry half of the blanched potatoes at a time in the oil for 2 to 3 minutes or until golden and crispy. Watch out for splattering. Drain on the second baking sheet. Season with salt. Keep the fries warm in the oven while you fry the remaining potatoes.

POTATOES We tested several varieties and settled on the regular white potato, which is versatile and suitable for all uses. However, you can also go with other varieties, such as a russet for crispier fries, Yukon Gold for its sweet taste or red-skinned potatoes for fries reminiscent of your favorite burger spot.

SOAKING This is an important step in order to rid the potatoes of their starch. After you've cut the potatoes, rinse and then immerse them in a bowl of cold water for a minimum of 30 minutes. The potatoes will absorb the water, making your fries crispier, with a consistent golden color and without the grainy texture of the starch.

SMOKY TASTE After trying out different kinds of oils (peanut, olive, canola) and animal fats (duck fat, lard), we decided on canola oil as the best choice for frying. It's also one of the more affordable oils. Given its neutral taste, we flavored it with bacon slices, which gave the fries an enjoyable smoky taste, similar to old school fries that were cooked in tallow (fat rendered from beef).

DOUBLE FRY This recipe is cooked twice: the potatoes are first blanched at a low temperature (300°F/150°C), until lightly golden. Once cooled until firm and no longer mealy, they're then fried once more in hot oil (350°F/180°C) until crispy.

Caesar Salad

PREPARATION 25 minutes
COOKING 12 minutes
SERVINGS 4

Croutons

2 cups	(100 g) diced day-old white bread with crusts removed
¼ cup	(55 g) butter

Capers

2 tbsp	capers, drained and patted dry
1 tbsp	(15 ml) olive oil

Mayonnaise

2	egg yolks
2 tbsp	(30 ml) lemon juice
1 tsp	chopped anchovy fillets
1 pinch	finely chopped garlic
¼ cup	(60 ml) vegetable oil
¼ cup	(60 ml) olive oil

Salad

8 cups	(360 g) torn romaine lettuce heart leaves
⅓ cup	(25 g) finely grated fresh Parmesan cheese
¼ cup	(30 g) Parmesan cheese shavings
8	slices cooked bacon, chopped

Croutons

With the rack in the middle position, preheat the oven to 325°F (165°C).

In an ovenproof skillet over medium heat, brown the bread in the butter. Season with salt. Transfer to the oven and bake for 6 minutes or until the croutons are crispy.

Capers

Meanwhile, in a small skillet over medium-high heat, fry the capers in the oil for 5 minutes or until very crispy. Drain on a plate lined with paper towels. On a work surface, finely chop half of the capers. Set the whole capers aside.

Mayonnaise

In a bowl, whisk the egg yolks with the lemon juice, anchovies, garlic and chopped capers. Slowly drizzle in the vegetable oil and olive oil, whisking constantly, until the mixture emulsifies and thickens. Season with salt and pepper.

Salad

In a large bowl, combine the lettuce, grated Parmesan, three-quarters of the Parmesan shavings, three-quarters of the bacon and three-quarters of the croutons. Add the mayonnaise and mix well.

Divide the salad among four plates. Garnish with the remaining Parmesan shavings, bacon, croutons and the reserved fried capers.

GOLDEN CROUTONS You want small bread cubes that are perfectly golden and crunchy, so you'll need to cook them twice, first in a skillet to brown the exterior and then in the oven to properly cook the inside.

A TOUCH OF GARLIC This is an essential ingredient, but resist the urge to overuse it, otherwise you'll burn your taste buds. The recipe only requires a small amount.

PARMESAN TWO WAYS We chose to use finely grated cheese that can be sprinkled everywhere but also large curls to enhance the presentation and that are simply a joy to bite into!

FRIED CAPERS Capers are what distinguish our best salad from our classic version. These briny little buds, fried whole in oil, explode with flavor and bring a lightly crispy, enjoyable texture when you bite into them. Of course we also chose to set a few aside to chop into the mayonnaise.

TWO OILS The Caesar salad's success rests on a good balance of flavors. This principle applies to the mayonnaise as well, which is why we chose equal parts olive oil, for its rich taste, and vegetable oil, for its lightness.

Gazpacho

PREPARATION 30 minutes
COOKING 5 minutes
CHILLING 2 hours
SERVINGS 4

Soup

1½ cups	(75 g) cubed day-old country bread with crusts removed
½ cup	(125 ml) water
2¼ lb	(1 kg) very ripe tomatoes, blanched, peeled, seeded and coarsely chopped
¾	English cucumber, peeled, seeded and cubed
¾	red bell pepper, seeded and cubed
2	green onions
½ cup	(125 ml) olive oil
2 tbsp	(30 ml) sherry vinegar or red wine vinegar

Toppings

1 cup	(50 g) diced day-old country bread with crusts removed
1 tbsp	(15 ml) olive oil, plus more for serving
¼	English cucumber, seeded and cut into small dice
¼	red bell pepper, seeded and cut into small dice

Soup

In a bowl, soak the cubed bread in the water for 5 minutes. Transfer to a blender. Add the tomatoes, cucumber, bell pepper, green onions, olive oil and vinegar and purée until smooth. Season with salt and pepper.

Refrigerate for 2 hours or until the soup has completely chilled.

Toppings

Meanwhile, in a large non-stick skillet over medium-high heat, brown the bread in the oil. Drain the croutons on a plate lined with paper towels. Let cool.

Divide the gazpacho among four bowls. Garnish with the croutons, cucumber and bell pepper. Drizzle with olive oil.

BREAD CHOICE Bread is the ideal ingredient when it comes to thickening and binding together a gazpacho. It also gives a creamy texture and accentuates the flavor. We first tried using store-bought sliced white bread but quickly realized that artisanal country bread, with its more pronounced flavor, enhanced both the soup and the crouton garnish.

SWEET PEPPER In contrast to the classic Spanish version, here we replace the green pepper, which provides an herby flavor, with a red pepper for its natural sweetness. It's a great way to enhance the color of the soup and also to help balance the acidity of the tomatoes.

RIPE TOMATOES They're the key ingredient to this raw vegetable-based soup, which can be considered a liquid salad! We avoid using canned tomatoes and prefer those that are in season, red and perfectly ripe. The best ones are available between July and September. It's also imperative to blanch, peel and seed the tomatoes before use, because the skin creates an unpleasant texture and the seeds can give a bitter taste to the soup.

Homemade Chunky Ketchup

PREPARATION 1 hour 15 minutes
COOKING 1 hour 30 minutes
COOLING 2 hours
MAKES 16 cups (4 L)
FREEZES WELL

2 tbsp	pickling spices
24	plum tomatoes, blanched, peeled and diced
12	apples, peeled, cored and diced
6	onions, diced
1	red bell pepper, seeded and diced
1	green bell pepper, seeded and diced
5 cups	(1 kg) sugar
2 cups	(500 ml) white vinegar
2 tbsp	fine salt

Place the pickling spices in a tea ball or double layer of cheesecloth.

In a large, heavy-bottomed pot, combine the pickling spices, tomatoes, apples, onions, red and green bell peppers, sugar, vinegar and salt. Bring to a boil, stirring often.

Simmer, uncovered, over medium heat for 1 hour 15 minutes, stirring occasionally. Remove and compost the pickling spices.

Pour the ketchup into hot sterilized jars. Let cool. Seal and refrigerate. Delicious served with Chicken Pot Pie (p. 98).

| NOTE | To make the jars shelf-stable after filling with ketchup, boil them in water for 15 minutes. The boiled jars will keep for 1 year at room temperature. Non-boiled jars will keep for 3 weeks in the refrigerator or 3 months in the freezer.

WITH OR WITHOUT VINEGAR? We prefer a tangy, well-balanced ketchup. Adding vinegar to the ketchup helps keep the chunky shape and crunchy texture of the fruits and vegetables it's made with. The acidity of the vinegar reacts with the pectin in the fruit, keeping it from softening.

PULPY TOMATOES We use plum tomatoes for this chunky ketchup because they're not too juicy, giving them a better pulp-to-water ratio, and they contain few seeds.

CLASSIC SPICES There's something nostalgic about using pickling spices, so we stay true to this childhood aroma for our ketchup. And, sticking with the nostalgia theme, we use the same trick as our mothers: wrapping them in a piece of cheesecloth (but a tea infuser ball also works well).

A TOUCH OF SUGAR 5 cups of sugar are essential to obtain the perfect texture for this ketchup. It may seem like a lot, but it's necessary to slow down the softening of the fruit. Not to mention the fact that sugar helps with preservation too.

Pea Soup

PREPARATION 20 minutes
SOAKING 1 hour
COOKING 2 hours 15 minutes
WAITING 1 hour
SERVINGS 4
FREEZES WELL

1½ cups	(310 g) whole yellow peas, rinsed and drained
1	tsp baking soda
¼ lb	(115 g) bacon, finely chopped
1	carrot, cut into small dice
1	large onion, finely chopped
4 cups	(1 L) chicken broth
3 cups	(750 ml) water
2	bay leaves

Place the yellow peas in a small pot and cover with cold water. Bring to a boil. Simmer for 2 minutes. Remove from the heat.

Add the baking soda to the pot. Mix and let soak for 1 hour at room temperature. Add water, as needed, so the peas are always covered. Rinse and drain the peas. Discard the soaking water.

In a large pot over high heat, cook the bacon until nicely browned. Add the carrot and onion. Cook over medium heat for 5 minutes or until the vegetables are translucent.

Add the peas, broth, water and bay leaves to the pot. Season generously with pepper. Bring to a boil. Cover and simmer for 2 hours (see note) or until the peas are tender and about half of them have burst. The soup will have started to thicken but should still be liquid. Adjust the seasoning. Remove and compost the bay leaves.

Let the soup sit for 1 hour before serving to obtain the desired consistency. The soup is best enjoyed the following day or freeze at this point, if desired. When ready to reheat, add a bit of water or broth to thin out the soup as needed.

| NOTE | If doubling the recipe, increase the cooking time to 3 hours.

BACON OR PORK BELLY? Although salt pork is traditionally used in pea soup, we use bacon for this recipe instead. It adds a smokiness that pork belly simply does not have, helping to flavor the broth. Given that the bacon is already salted, avoid adding any more salt to the recipe and only adjust the seasoning at the very end, if needed.

THE PEA-FECT CHOICE The choice of peas for this recipe wasn't a minor one. Many versions use split yellow peas, but we find they tend to get pretty mushy, practically turning into a purée. Instead, we opted for whole peas, which hold up better when cooked and add more texture to the soup, even though they cook more slowly.

SOAK IT ALL UP To avoid being left with hard peas even after they've been cooking for a while, try the soaking technique of this recipe, using baking soda in boiling water. In addition to reducing soaking time to just an hour (as opposed to overnight), it makes the peas very tender. Be sure to rinse them well before cooking.

MUCH-NEEDED REST It's usual for the soup to be very liquid as it cooks, but after a period of rest, the peas will absorb a good amount of the liquid. We suggest waiting until the next day to eat it. The cooling time will allow the soup to thicken and reach the optimal consistency.

Wonton Soup

PREPARATION 1 hour 15 minutes
MARINATING 15 minutes
COOKING 45 minutes
MAKES 6 appetizers
FREEZES WELL

Wontons

½ lb	(225 g) unpeeled medium shrimp (26–30), thawed
1 tsp	baking soda
¼ tsp	salt
¼ lb	(115 g) medium-lean ground pork
2 tbsp	(30 ml) low-sodium soy sauce
1 tbsp	(15 ml) Shaoxing rice wine, sherry or sake
1	green onion, thinly sliced
1½ tsp	finely grated fresh ginger
1 tsp	(5 ml) toasted sesame oil, plus more for serving
⅛ tsp	ground white pepper
30	frozen square wonton wrappers, thawed

Broth

8 cups	(2 L) water
2 lb	(900 g) chicken drumsticks or other bone-in chicken pieces (such as wings or carcasses)
4	green onions, white parts chopped and green parts thinly sliced
1	piece fresh ginger, about 1 inch (2.5 cm) long, sliced
2 tsp	brown sugar
2 tsp	salt
1 tbsp	(15 ml) fish sauce
⅛ tsp	ground white pepper

Wontons

On a work surface, shell and devein the shrimp. Set the shells aside in the refrigerator for the broth. Cut 6 shrimp into 5 pieces each and place in a bowl. Add the baking soda and salt. Mix well. Let marinate for 15 minutes.

Rinse the chopped shrimp under cold running water. Drain and pat very dry with paper towels. Cover and refrigerate.

Meanwhile, on a work surface, chop the remaining shrimp and place in another bowl. Add the pork, soy sauce, rice wine, green onion, ginger, sesame oil and pepper. Mix well. Cover and refrigerate while you prepare the broth.

Broth

In a large pot, place the water, chicken, reserved shrimp shells, white parts of the green onions, ginger, brown sugar and salt. Bring to a boil, skimming as needed. Simmer for 25 minutes.

Remove the chicken from the pot and set aside for another use. Strain the broth through a fine sieve set over a large bowl. Compost the aromatics. Wash out the pot.

Return the broth to the clean pot. Add the fish sauce and white pepper. Adjust the seasoning. Keep the broth warm or freeze at this point, if desired.

Assembly

Meanwhile, on a work surface, lay out 4 wonton wrappers. Place 1 tsp of the pork filling in the center of each square. Place 1 piece of shrimp over the pork filling. Using a pastry brush, moisten two adjacent sides of each wrapper with water and fold over toward the opposite sides to form a triangle. Press together to seal around the filling. Moisten one of the tips on the longer side of the triangle and pinch together with the opposite tip to seal. Place the wontons on a baking sheet lined with parchment paper and cover the wontons with a kitchen towel as you go to prevent them drying out.

Repeat with the remaining wrappers, pork filling and shrimp pieces. Freeze the wontons at this point, if desired. Once the raw wontons are frozen, transfer them to an airtight container. They will keep in the freezer for 3 months. They can be cooked from frozen for roughly the same amount of time as when cooked fresh.

In a large pot of boiling salted water, cook the wontons for 5 minutes. Using a slotted spoon, remove the wontons from the water and divide among six serving bowls. Top with the hot broth. Drizzle each serving with sesame oil and sprinkle with the green parts of the green onions.

DIFFERENT TEXTURES To keep the filling from being too compact and dense, we use different textures of meat. We also prefer cutting some of the shrimp into chunks and finely chopping the rest. Including ground pork in the mixture gives the best result.

MAGIC POWDER Among the ingredients that help create textural contrast is baking soda, which is used to coat the shrimp pieces. This makes them more plump, and keeps them distinct from the rest of the filling.

EASY FOLDING We choose to use frozen store-bought wrappers for these wontons; neither too thin nor too thick, they allow for folding that's similar to tortellini. This ensures more even cooking, a compact filling and an elegant result.

LIGHT BROTH Given that the wontons are packed with flavor, they require just a light broth to go along with them. This broth is made using chicken drumsticks and shrimp shells, which have a delicate flavor, and the addition of ginger and brown sugar contributes to its delicious aroma.

Tzatziki

PREPARATION 20 minutes
CHILLING 4 hours
MAKES about 2 cups (500 ml)

2 cups	(500 ml) 10% plain yogurt
1	English cucumber, peeled and seeded
1 tbsp	(15 ml) white wine vinegar
½ tsp	salt
2	garlic cloves, finely grated
¼ cup	(60 ml) olive oil, plus more for serving
2 tbsp	finely chopped dill, plus more for serving
1 tbsp	finely chopped mint leaves, plus more for serving
1 pinch	dried oregano
1	kalamata olive (optional)
	Thick pita bread or sliced baguette, for serving

Line a large fine sieve with a layer of paper towels or three layers of cheesecloth and place over a large bowl.

Pour the yogurt into the sieve. Cover with paper towels or fold the cheesecloth over to cover the yogurt. Let drain in the refrigerator for 4 to 8 hours or until the yogurt is firm and about ½ cup (125 ml) of liquid has accumulated in the bowl. Discard the liquid.

Grate the cucumber on the largest side of a box grater. In a bowl, combine the grated cucumber with the vinegar and salt. Let sit for 10 minutes. Drain the cucumber by pressing it into a sieve or squeezing it between your hands.

In a bowl, combine the strained yogurt, grated cucumber, garlic, oil, dill and mint. Mix vigorously for 2 minutes until well combined and emulsified. Season with salt and pepper.

Serve the tzatziki in a shallow bowl. Drizzle with olive oil and sprinkle with dried oregano. Top with the kalamata olive and a sprinkling of fresh herbs. Serve with lightly toasted thick pita or slices of baguette.

RICH IN FAT A good tzatziki should be rich and creamy. For this reason, we dismissed all yogurts labeled 0% fat; their texture is often rather chalky. Instead, we use 10% yogurt and make sure to strain it.

CUCUMBER PREP Cucumbers have a high water content, so it's important to drain any excess water. We recommend peeling and seeding to avoid any bitterness, but you can keep the skin on if it's thin, as well as the seeds if they're small.

POWERFUL GARLIC Raw, biting garlic needs to stand out in this recipe, without you literally biting into pieces, so we grate it into a fine paste using a zester. For a less overwhelming garlic taste, refrigerate your tzatziki for a few hours before serving.

AN HERBY PAIR Many versions of this dish exist, some without herbs, others with either dill or mint. We decided to combine the two for added freshness and a touch of summer.

OPTIMAL TEXTURE By straining the grated cucumber and yogurt, you can remove ¾ cup (180 ml) of liquid from the tzatziki; adding oil helps it reach a firmer, well-emulsified texture and contributes to the overall taste.

Fully Loaded Baked Potatoes

PREPARATION 40 minutes
COOKING 45 minutes
SERVINGS 4 to 8

4	large russet potatoes, scrubbed clean
4	slices bacon
¼ cup	(55 g) butter, softened
1 cup	(250 ml) sour cream
1½ cups	(150 g) grated orange or white cheddar cheese
2	green onions, white parts chopped and green parts thinly sliced

Preheat the grill, setting the burners to high.

Individually wrap each potato with foil. Place on the grill. Close the lid of the barbecue and cook for 30 to 40 minutes or until the potatoes are tender, turning them over regularly during cooking. Let cool slightly.

At the same time, place the bacon on the grill around the potatoes and cook for 2 to 3 minutes on each side or until crispy. Drain on a plate lined with paper towels. On a work surface, finely chop the bacon. Set aside in a bowl.

On a work surface, arrange the potatoes horizontally and cut off the tops. Set the tops aside for another use. Scoop out the flesh from each potato, leaving about ½ inch (1 cm) of flesh all around. Set aside the flesh and potato skins separately.

In another bowl, purée the potato flesh with a potato ricer or masher. Add the butter, sour cream, 1 cup (100 g) of the cheddar, the white parts of the green onions and half of the chopped bacon. Season with salt and pepper. Mix well.

Generously fill the potato skins with the mashed potato mixture. Sprinkle with the remaining cheddar, bacon and green parts of the green onions.

Reduce the heat of the barbecue to medium. Place the stuffed potatoes directly on the grill. Close the lid and cook for 15 to 20 minutes or until the cheese has melted.

POTATOES Russet is our top choice of potato here, as a starchy variety with a light and flaky texture that absorbs fats well. Its length makes it great for loading it up with fillings too, and its thick skin is hard to pierce while scooping out its insides.

COOKED TWICE Cook the potatoes first wrapped in aluminum foil to keep them from drying out, while making them soft and perfectly cooked. Then, toss them onto the grill for a perfectly crisp texture.

FAT For a creamy and gourmet potato skin, we use sour cream. Its smooth texture and tanginess go well with the delicate potato flesh, and its natural creaminess allows you to use less butter in the filling.

ESSENTIAL TOPPINGS We didn't stray from tradition here but went with classic toppings: Crispy bacon for its smoky taste; mild green onion for its texture and flavor; and mild cheddar that melts well and doesn't mask the taste of the potato.

Fried Calamari

PREPARATION 35 minutes
COOKING 10 minutes
SERVINGS 4

Aioli

2	egg yolks
1 tbsp	(15 ml) Dijon mustard
1	small garlic clove, finely chopped
¾ cup	(180 ml) equal parts vegetable oil and olive oil
2 tbsp	(30 ml) water
1 tbsp	(15 ml) lemon juice

Calamari

¾ lb	(340 g) whole squid (see note)
	Vegetable oil, for frying
¾ cup	(25 g) crispy rice cereal
¾ cup	(115 g) unbleached all-purpose flour
¾ cup	(90 g) corn flour
¼ tsp	sweet paprika
¼ tsp	cayenne pepper
¼ tsp	salt
2	egg whites
	Lemon wedges, for serving

Aioli

In a bowl, whisk together the egg yolks, mustard and garlic. Slowly drizzle in one-third of the oil, whisking constantly. When the emulsion starts to resemble mayonnaise, drizzle in the remaining oil while continuing to whisk. Season with pepper. Stir in the water and lemon juice.

Transfer the aioli to a small bowl and refrigerate until ready to serve.

Calamari

On a work surface, separate the squid heads from the bodies. Using a knife, cut the heads and remove the beaks. Pull the cartilage out of each body. Peel off the fins and skin, if desired. Rinse the squid parts under cold running water. Pat very dry with paper towels. Cut the bodies into rings ½ inch (1 cm) thick. Refrigerate.

Preheat the oil in a deep fryer to 365°F (185°C). Line a baking sheet with paper towels or a wire rack. Preheat the oven to 200°F (95°C).

In a small food processor, pulse the cereal until the size of fine breadcrumbs. Transfer to a bowl. Add the all-purpose flour, corn flour, paprika, cayenne and salt. Mix well.

In another bowl, whisk the egg whites until frothy.

Dip the squid pieces in the egg whites, letting some of the excess drip off. Press a few pieces at a time in the breadcrumb mixture to coat well, shaking off any excess.

Fry a few pieces at a time in the hot oil for 1 minute or until golden. Watch out for splattering. Drain on the baking sheet. Keep warm in the oven on another baking sheet while you fry the remaining squid.

Serve the calamari with lemon wedges and the aioli.

| NOTE | **Whether your squid is cleaned already or not, rinsing it under cold running water and patting very dry is an important step before cooking.**

FRESHNESS REIGNS A marinade isn't what makes calamari tender; it's the squid's freshness and quality that gives optimal results.

BEST BREADING After many attempts we eventually landed on a blend of equal parts crushed puffed rice cereal, all-purpose flour and corn flour. This provides a crisp yet light texture and a wonderfully golden color—plus it tastes perfectly seasoned after the addition of paprika and cayenne pepper.

LIGHTWEIGHT EGG WHITE Using an egg wash with whole egg made for a coating that felt heavy, but egg whites provided an airier texture. And it works out well, given that we have whites left over after using the yolks for the aioli!

LEMONY SAUCE Many swear by a tomato-based marinara sauce or simply a drizzle of lemon juice for fried calamari, but we love this garlic and lemon aioli sauce for its freshness and creaminess.

Hummus

PREPARATION 30 minutes
SOAKING 12 hours
COOKING 1 hour
MAKES 3 cups (750 ml)

Chickpeas

1 cup	(205 g) dried chickpeas

Hummus

12⅓ cups	(3.075 L) water
1 tsp	baking soda
5	garlic cloves, halved
½ cup	(125 ml) tahini
6 tbsp	(90 ml) lemon juice
1 tsp	salt
¼ tsp	ground cumin
⅛ tsp	cayenne pepper

Toppings

2 tbsp	(30 ml) olive oil
1 tsp	finely chopped flat-leaf parsley
	Roasted cumin seeds, to taste
	Roasted sesame seeds, to taste
	Ground sumac, to taste

Chickpeas

Place the chickpeas in a large bowl and cover with cold water. Let soak for 12 hours or overnight at room temperature. Add water as needed, so the chickpeas are always covered. Rinse and drain.

Hummus

In a pot, bring the chickpeas, 12 cups (3 L) of the water and the baking soda to a boil. Skim the surface as needed. Reduce the heat and simmer for 25 minutes.

Using a slotted spoon, remove 10 chickpeas from the pot and set aside in a bowl to use as decoration, if desired. Continue to cook the remaining chickpeas for 15 minutes.

Add the garlic to the pot and continue to cook for 10 minutes. Drain the chickpeas and garlic. Let cool on a baking sheet. Remove as many skins as you can from the cooled chickpeas.

In a food processor, purée the tahini while gradually adding the remaining ⅓ cup (75 ml) water until very creamy. Gradually add in the lemon juice. Add the chickpeas, salt, cumin and cayenne. Purée again until very smooth, about 3 minutes. Using a spatula, scrape down the sides of the food processor as needed. Transfer to a bowl. Cover and refrigerate until ready to serve.

Toppings

Transfer the hummus to a serving bowl or shallow dish, making decorative waves in the surface with a spoon. Drizzle with the oil, letting it fall between the waves in the surface. Garnish with the parsley, cumin and sesame seeds, sumac and reserved chickpeas. Season with pepper. Serve with pita, if desired.

CHICKPEAS To make the best hummus, use dried chickpeas instead of canned. The advantage of cooking the chickpeas after they've soaked overnight is that you can control the cooking process. They'll also have a milder taste, without that metallic tang normally found in canned goods.

CREAMINESS One of the key elements of a good hummus is its creamy consistency. Given that they can keep your hummus from achieving a smooth texture, we highly recommend removing as many of the chickpea skins as possible by hand once cooked before blending the ingredients in the food processor.

SOAKING Baking soda helps to tenderize the chickpeas more quickly and releases their outer skins, but when we tried soaking the chickpeas in a baking soda and water solution, it made the chickpeas burst while cooking. The trick is to add the baking soda to the cooking water instead of the soaking water.

BLANCHED GARLIC The taste of garlic overpowers the hummus if added right before blending. Instead, we blanch a few cloves in the water with the chickpeas toward the end of the cooking process. This way, the garlic's pronounced flavor is softened and reveals itself gradually. There's also a touch of heat from the cayenne pepper, which suits the dish better than peppercorns.

Fried Onion Rings

PREPARATION 30 minutes
COOKING 25 minutes
SERVINGS 4 to 6
FREEZES WELL

Onions

	Vegetable oil, for frying
2	Vidalia onions, peeled

Coating

1 cup	(150 g) unbleached all-purpose flour
⅓ cup	(55 g) rice flour
½ tsp	salt
½ tsp	sweet paprika
¼ tsp	cayenne pepper

Batter

1 cup	(150 g) unbleached all-purpose flour
½ tsp	baking powder
½ tsp	salt
½ tsp	sweet paprika
¼ tsp	cayenne pepper
1 cup	(250 ml) light pale ale, cold
2 tbsp	(30 ml) ice water

Onions

Preheat the oil in a deep fryer to 365°F (185°C). Line a baking sheet with paper towels or a wire rack. Preheat the oven to 200°F (95°C).

On a work surface, cut the onions into rounds ½ inch (1 cm) thick. Separate into rings. Set the smaller pieces aside for another use.

Coating

In a bowl, combine all of the ingredients. Set aside.

Batter

In a large bowl, combine the flour, baking powder, salt, paprika and cayenne. Whisk in the beer and water until smooth.

Dip a few onion rings at a time in the beer batter, shaking off any excess. Dredge in the coating and place on another baking sheet as you go. Freeze at this point, if desired (see note). As you work, strain the coating through a sieve to remove any lumps, as needed, and compost them.

Fry a few onion rings at a time until golden, turning them over halfway through, about 3 minutes. Watch out for splattering. Drain on the prepared baking sheet. Season with salt.

Keep warm in the oven while you fry the remaining onion rings.

| NOTE | **Freeze the onion rings on a baking sheet lined with parchment paper, making sure they aren't touching. Once they are completely frozen, transfer them to an airtight container. They will keep for 1 month in the freezer. You can fry them from frozen for the same amount of time.**

PERFECT ONIONS The Vidalia onion was the big winner when it came to developing this recipe. Large and slightly flattened, it yields rings of a good size and standard shape, and we also enjoy its sweet taste, as opposed to the strong taste of yellow onions. They can easily be found at the grocery store, sold in bags or individually.

BEER EFFECT Adding beer to the fry batter, along with baking powder, helps the batter expand, making for a light and airy coating. We recommend a blond ale, like a lager or a pilsner, because it's light and doesn't have any bitterness. For the ideal reaction when it comes into contact with the hot oil, the beer must be cold up until the moment you pour it in.

CRISPY COATING Rice flour aerates the all-purpose flour in the coating, but still brings crunch to the breading. We included paprika and cayenne pepper for color and a kick of flavor (but you can omit the spices for a more neutral flavor). You can use this batter and technique with other vegetables for frying.

QUICK COOK We use a deep fryer for this recipe because we don't find the air fryer yields the same results. For perfectly cooked onion rings, fry the rings in oil for 2 minutes 30 seconds to 3 minutes at most. The oil must remain at a high temperature throughout; make sure it doesn't cool between each batch of rings.

Buffalo Chicken Wings

PREPARATION 30 minutes
COOKING 36 minutes
SERVINGS 6 to 8 appetizers
FREEZES WELL

Chicken Wings

	Vegetable oil, for frying
12	chicken wings (see note)
3 tbsp	cornstarch
1 tsp	salt
1 tsp	chili powder
¼ tsp	cayenne pepper
¼ tsp	onion powder

Sauce

¼ cup	(55 g) butter
½ cup	(125 ml) hot sauce (see note)
2 tbsp	brown sugar
1 tbsp	(15 ml) apple cider vinegar

Chicken Wings

Preheat the oil in a deep fryer to 350°F (180°C). Line a baking sheet with paper towels or a wire rack. Preheat the oven to 200°F (95°C).

On a work surface, cut each chicken wing through the joints into three pieces. Compost the wing tips and keep only the two large pieces. Pat the wings dry with paper towels.

In a large bowl, combine the cornstarch, salt, chili powder, cayenne and onion powder. Add the chicken wings and toss to coat. Fry a few wings at a time for 12 to 15 minutes or until cooked through and nicely browned. Watch out for splattering. Drain on the baking sheet. Keep warm in the oven while you fry the remaining wings.

Sauce

Meanwhile, in a small pot, combine the butter, hot sauce, sugar and vinegar. Bring to a boil. Simmer over low heat for 5 minutes or until the sauce has reduced by half. Pour into a large bowl. Add the cooked wings and toss to coat well with the sauce.

Serve immediately with blue cheese dip and celery sticks, if desired.

| NOTES | Chicken wings are sold whole or in pieces. If they are whole, you will need to separate them into pieces as described above. Regardless of how you buy them, you will need a total of 24 pieces.

We use Frank's RedHot sauce, which is ideal for Buffalo wings. It's spicy without being too hot and has just the right amount of tang and acidity.

VERY CRISPY The main issue when it comes to making Buffalo wings is that of texture: they need to be as crispy as possible. And to achieve that you need to fry them in oil. Once out of the deep fryer, they'll be wonderfully crispy on the outside, and the meat inside will be perfectly juicy.

CLASSIC INGREDIENTS When it comes to chicken wings, there's no better accompaniment than a smooth homemade sauce. For a maximum of flavor, you need just four ingredients: brown sugar for sweetness, vinegar for tanginess, butter for richness, and of course, hot sauce for that kick of heat.

PERFECT COATING One challenge we had was figuring out the right moment to coat the wings. We tried both before and after placing the wings in the oven. Before, the sauce didn't stay on the wings, melting onto the baking sheet while in the oven. After, and it coated them to perfection. A metal mixing bowl is best to help coat the wings in the sauce.

JUST ENOUGH HEAT Once fried, it's important to place the chicken wings onto paper towels to absorb the cooking oil. This helps ensure that the sauce adheres well to the wings. When you bite into that first wing, you may feel like it isn't hot enough. It's only once you have a third or fourth wing that its real flavor will reveal itself, with a surprising and satisfying heat!

French Onion Soup

PREPARATION 20 minutes
COOKING 1 hour 5 minutes
SERVINGS 4
BROTH FREEZES WELL

Soup

6	yellow onions, peeled
¼ cup	(55 g) butter
½ cup	(125 ml) red wine
2 tbsp	(30 ml) cognac or brandy
4 cups	(1 L) chicken broth
4 cups	(1 L) beef broth
1 tbsp	light toasted flour
1 pinch	ground nutmeg

Toppings

12	slices baguette, each about ½ inch (1 cm) thick, toasted
1	small garlic clove, halved
2 cups	(200 g) grated Gruyère cheese

Soup

On a work surface, quarter the onions. Thinly slice each quarter widthwise to get short strips.

In a large pot over medium heat, soften the onions in the butter for 15 minutes, stirring occasionally.

Continue to cook over high heat for 15 minutes or until the onions are caramelized, stirring constantly and scraping the bottom of the pot. Deglaze with the wine and cognac. Let reduce until almost dry. Add the chicken broth, beef broth, toasted flour and nutmeg. Mix well.

Bring the soup to a boil. Simmer over medium-high heat for 30 minutes or until reduced by half. You should have about 5 cups (1.25 L) of soup. Season with salt and pepper. Freeze at this point, if desired.

Toppings

With the rack in the middle position, preheat the oven to broil. Place four ovenproof bowls on a baking sheet.

Meanwhile, lightly rub each slice of toast with the cut-side of the garlic clove. Divide the soup among the bowls and top each one with 2 tbsp of the Gruyère. Place 3 pieces of garlic toast in each bowl and sprinkle with the remaining Gruyère.

Broil for 5 minutes or until the cheese is melted and golden.

PREFERRED ONION Multipurpose yellow onions that you likely already have in your pantry yield the best results. When browning them, cook them slowly for a beautiful caramelization.

CHOICE OF ALCOHOL To deglaze, we prefer red wine by a long shot, with a touch of cognac or brandy. The former brings structure to the soup, while the latter enriches it.

DELICIOUS BROTH We use both beef and chicken broths for this soup, because each provides its own unique flavor: beef for its full-bodiedness and chicken for its balance. Toasted flour is added to intensify the flavors along with a pinch of nutmeg that adds complexity to the dish and enhances the taste of the cheese.

BAGUETTE As a topping, we went with baguette. Its crust-to-crumb ratio is perfect, and it easily absorbs the broth. Place the slices on top at the last moment so that they brown directly in the soup. We recommend rubbing each slice with a garlic clove half; it's a small gesture that makes a big difference.

Minestrone Soup

PREPARATION 35 minutes
COOKING 1 hour 15 minutes
SERVINGS 6
FREEZES WELL

1	onion, diced
1	carrot, diced
1	celery stalk, diced
3 tbsp	(45 ml) olive oil, plus more for serving
1	zucchini, diced
4	garlic cloves, finely chopped
4 cups	(1 L) chicken broth
2 cups	(500 ml) water
½ lb	(225 g) green beans, trimmed and cut into pieces ½ inch (1 cm) long
2 cups	(170 g) thinly sliced Savoy cabbage
1 cup	(160 g) peeled and diced potatoes
1 can	(19 oz/540 ml) white beans, rinsed and drained
1 can	(14 oz/398 ml) diced tomatoes
2	bay leaves
1	Parmesan cheese rind
¾ cup	(105 g) small pasta shells
	Grated fresh Parmesan cheese, for serving

In a pot over medium-high heat, cook the onion, carrot and celery in the oil for 8 minutes or until translucent. Season with salt.

Add the zucchini and garlic to the pot. Continue to cook for 5 minutes or until the zucchini is lightly browned. Add the broth, water, green beans, cabbage, potatoes, beans, tomatoes, bay leaves and Parmesan rind. Season with salt and pepper. Bring to a boil. Simmer for 45 minutes or until the vegetables are tender and the soup has thickened slightly.

Meanwhile, in another pot of boiling salted water, cook the pasta until tender (see note). Drain.

Add the pasta to the soup. Remove and compost the bay leaves and Parmesan rind. Adjust the seasoning.

Divide the soup among six bowls. Drizzle with oil and sprinkle with grated Parmesan. Serve with basil pesto or bread, if desired.

| NOTE | For a soup with a lot of broth, the pasta has to first cook long enough to be soft and not al dente, which is the usual suggested doneness for pasta. If al dente, the pasta will absorb too much of the liquid from the soup.

VEGETABLE SIZE The size of your vegetables is important in this soup. Cut them into small, similarly sized pieces for easy and even cooking. This recipe follows a precise order, beginning with an aromatic base known as sofrito, a trio used in Italian recipes consisting of carrots, celery and onions.

CANNED TOMATOES We set aside the fresh tomatoes for this recipe because of their acidity and chose canned diced tomatoes instead. They're already cooked and peeled, and you can find a bit of purée at the bottom of the can, which helps to thicken the broth and concentrate the flavors.

SATISFYINGLY STARCHY Minestrone is a hearty soup; using starches like diced potatoes, beans and pasta adds texture and also helps to thicken the broth.

SIMPLE FLAVORS To allow the vegetables to shine, we don't get too heavy-handed with the seasonings. We use just bay leaf, salt, pepper and a secret ingredient: a Parmesan cheese rind, which adds depth to the dish. You may also serve this with pesto, which is customary in certain regions in Italy.

Mashed Potatoes

PREPARATION 15 minutes
COOKING 40 minutes
SERVINGS 4

6 cups	(1 kg) peeled and cubed Yukon Gold potatoes
8	garlic cloves, peeled
½ cup	(115 g) butter
½ cup	(125 ml) milk
	Seasoned brown butter (see note) or cubed butter (optional)

Place the potatoes and garlic in a pot. Cover with cold water and season with salt. Bring to a boil. Simmer for 25 minutes or until the potatoes are tender and fall apart easily when pierced with a fork. Drain. Return to the pot.

Using a potato masher, purée the potatoes and garlic with the butter. Gradually add the milk and mix until smooth (see note). Season with salt and pepper.

Serve in individual bowls. Just before serving, add a drizzle of seasoned brown butter or a cube of butter.

| **NOTES** | To make seasoned brown butter, melt ½ cup (115 g) butter in a small pot over medium heat. Add 2 peeled and halved garlic cloves, 2 bay leaves, 1 thyme sprig and 1 whole clove. Cook until the butter starts to brown and stops foaming. Immediately pour into a bowl. Do not strain. Season with pepper. Keep warm until ready to serve.

If preparing the mashed potatoes in advance, add a little extra milk to make them slightly runnier than you normally would. Mashed potatoes tend to thicken up as they rest.

A POTATO AFFAIR We highly recommend the Yukon Gold variety, which is lightly sweet and fragrant, enhancing the taste of the fats. It's no accident that we added an aromatic brown butter to the mash, making this yellow potato shine in all its glory.

WITH A GRAIN OF SALT Adding salt before mashing can mask the natural flavor of the spud. Instead, we include it in the cooking water, with a ratio of 1½ tsp of salt to 4 cups (1 L) of water. Using water that's been salted reduces the need to adjust the seasoning at the end.

GARLIC CLOVE Flavoring the potatoes gently helps enhance the mash. For a subtle aroma, we suggest placing the garlic in the water; it'll cook alongside the potatoes. Once boiled, it easily blends in with the potatoes under the weight of the potato masher for a gourmet touch.

COOK WELL People tend to not boil their potatoes long enough, making for gluey results. When perfectly cooked, potatoes should be translucent and practically soaked in water. Drain and mash them immediately. If you wait too long, the potato pieces will harden, making it more difficult to achieve a smooth mash.

Scalloped Potatoes

PREPARATION 30 minutes
COOKING 1 hour 20 minutes
WAITING 15 minutes
SERVINGS 6 to 8

3 cups	(750 ml) milk
1 cup	(250 ml) 35% cream
1	onion, peeled and halved
3	garlic cloves, peeled and halved
4½ lb	(2 kg) white potatoes, peeled and cut into slices ⅛ inch (3 mm) thick on a mandoline
½ tsp	salt
1 cup	(100 g) grated Gruyère cheese

With the rack in the lowest position, preheat the oven to 400°F (200°C).

In a large pot, bring the milk, cream, onion and garlic to a boil. Simmer gently for 5 minutes. Remove and compost the onion and garlic.

Add the potatoes and salt to the pot. Bring to a boil. Simmer very gently for 15 minutes, delicately stirring several times. Stir in the Gruyère. Season with pepper. Transfer the mixture to a 9-inch (23 cm) square pan or an 11 × 8-inch (28 × 20 cm) rectangular baking dish.

Bake for 50 minutes or until the potatoes are tender and nicely browned. Let sit for 15 minutes before serving. This will make the potatoes easier to cut and serve.

When ready to serve the potatoes, season generously with pepper. Serve with a vinegary green salad and roasted meat (such as turkey, chicken, roast beef, veal, pork) if desired.

NO RINSING REQUIRED We choose not to rinse the potatoes after slicing them; their natural starchiness helps to maintain the dish's compact, silky and creamy texture.

PRECOOK POTATOES Precooking the potatoes makes them softer and allows the crust to get crispy—the dish also remains tightly packed and doesn't leak as it's baked.

CREAMY INFUSION For a more pronounced flavor, we infuse garlic and onion in the cream and remove them afterwards (rather than rub half a garlic clove on the bottom of the dish, as is common in the traditional version).

A BIT OF CHEESE Traditional scalloped potato recipes don't include cheese, but chefs like Bocuse and Robuchon include it in theirs and so do we! We prefer to use Gruyère, because it holds up well during baking—and we include it in the filling, rather than as a topping, to allow the potatoes and the cream to create a crispy, golden crust.

OTHER AROMAS Our recipe doesn't include nutmeg, because we prefer to preserve the mild taste of the potatoes and the subtleness of the cream and Gruyère cheese. If you choose to add some, use very little and make sure it's freshly grated. As for pepper, a quick twist of the grinder at the last minute will do the trick.

The Best Breakfasts

Thin Breakfast Crepes

PREPARATION 10 minutes
COOKING 25 minutes
SERVINGS 4
FREEZES WELL

1 cup	(150 g) unbleached all-purpose flour
2 tbsp	sugar
1 pinch	salt
2	eggs
1½ cups	(375 ml) milk
½ tsp	(2.5 ml) vanilla
1 tbsp	butter, melted, plus more for cooking

In a bowl, combine the flour, sugar and salt. Whisk in the eggs, ½ cup (125 ml) of the milk and the vanilla until smooth. Gradually whisk in the remaining milk. Whisk in the melted butter.

Heat a 9-inch (23 cm) non-stick skillet over medium heat. Once the skillet is hot, brush with butter.

For each crepe, pour about 3 tbsp (45 ml) of the batter into the center of the skillet. Tilt the skillet from side to side to spread the batter evenly to cover the entire bottom of the skillet. Once the edge of the crepe easily comes away from the skillet and starts to brown, flip it over using a spatula. Cook for another 10 seconds to brown slightly. Remove from the skillet.

Place the crepe on a plate and cover with foil. Keep warm in an oven preheated to 200°F (95°C) while you cook the remaining batter or serve them as you go. Delicious served with maple syrup.

BETTER BATTER To keep your batter from getting lumps, start by combining the dry ingredients with the eggs and only part of the milk. Add the rest of the milk once the batter is smooth. We use more milk than flour, to keep the batter thin and runny—with this ratio, the batter will spread out more evenly in the pan, yielding perfectly thin crepes.

FULL OF FLAVOR Because they are already a little sweet, these breakfast crepes are delicious served with jam, maple syrup and fruit. The sugar in the recipe helps the batter brown in the pan, while the vanilla brings the taste. Also, the pinch of salt shouldn't be omitted, as it elevates the flavors of the other ingredients.

PAN ON POINT Your lightly buttered pan needs to be hot before pouring in the batter, and more butter needs to be added with each new crepe. This allows for even caramelization and provides a satisfying brown butter taste.

KEEP ON FLIPPING Cooking transforms both the taste and color of the crepes. To develop a lightly toasted flavor, cook the first side up to three times as long as the second, which only requires a quick turn. The crepe is ready to be flipped when there is no trace of liquid left and it starts to brown lightly around the edges.

Pancakes

PREPARATION 10 minutes
COOKING 35 minutes
MAKES 8
FREEZES WELL

2 cups	(300 g) unbleached all-purpose flour
¼ cup	(55 g) sugar
2 tsp	baking powder
1 tsp	baking soda
¼ tsp	salt
2 cups	(500 ml) buttermilk (see note)
2	eggs
¼ cup	(55 g) unsalted butter, melted and cooled, plus more for cooking
1 tsp	(5 ml) vanilla

In a large bowl, combine the flour, sugar, baking powder, baking soda and salt.

In another bowl, combine the buttermilk, eggs, melted butter and vanilla.

Add the buttermilk mixture to the bowl of dry ingredients. Mix with a spatula just until the dry ingredients are moistened. Do not overmix the batter. A few clumps of flour should remain.

Warm a non-stick skillet over medium to low heat. Once the skillet is warm, brush with butter. For each pancake, pour about ½ cup (125 ml) of the batter into the center of the skillet. Using the back of a spoon, spread the batter out slightly.

Cook the pancake for 2 minutes on each side. It is ready to flip over when bubbles start to form at the center or when the edges are starting to cook. Adjust the heat as needed to allow the pancake time to cook before browning too quickly.

Keep the pancakes warm in an oven preheated to 200°F (95°C) while you cook the remaining batter or serve them as you go. Delicious served with maple syrup.

| NOTE | The buttermilk can be replaced with 2 cups (500 ml) milk mixed with 2 tbsp (30 ml) white vinegar or lemon juice. Let sit for 5 to 10 minutes. Stir before adding to the recipe. You could also use 1¼ cups (310 ml) plain yogurt mixed with ¾ cup (180 ml) milk.

BUTTERMILK Buttermilk is an asset to this recipe because it's an acid and it reacts with the baking soda and baking powder. By releasing carbon dioxide, it creates bubbles in the batter that'll make the pancakes light and airy, as whipped eggs would. It also adds a touch of tang and a milky taste to the batter. You can buy it in grocery stores or make it at home (see note above).

SWEET EFFECT Sugar adds sweetness to the batter but doesn't make it too sweet, as we like to add maple syrup and fruit afterwards. It also helps caramelize the perimeter of the pancakes as they cook, and to retain moisture in the batter, which keeps the pancakes soft on the inside.

DON'T OVERMIX We recommend not overmixing the batter to avoid developing the gluten too much, which leads to dense pancakes. Simply moisten the flour; there will be lumps, but that's okay. Baking soda and baking powder help to create air for extremely soft pancakes.

BUTTERY TASTE Not only does butter bring flavor to the pancakes, it also provides elasticity to the batter and stops them from drying out as they cook—making for even softer pancakes.

Scrambled Eggs

PREPARATION 5 minutes
COOKING 8 minutes
SERVINGS 6 to 8

12	eggs
¼ cup	(55 g) butter

In a bowl, whisk the eggs until smooth but not frothy. Season with salt and pepper.

In a medium pot or a large, deep skillet over medium-high heat, melt the butter. Pour in the eggs and stir gently with a spatula or wooden spoon, scraping the bottom and sides of the pot. Once the eggs begin to thicken, stir more rapidly until they are creamy and still runny (cook to about 80%, since the eggs will continue to cook off the heat). The eggs should now form small, moist clumps. Remove from the heat.

Adjust the seasoning. Transfer to a serving bowl. Serve immediately.

NO AIR Only eggs are required for this recipe, rather than milk too, which many people include. Make sure to mix the eggs well but without incorporating any air as air dries out the eggs once cooked. Simply break them up until they are uniform and not frothy.

WORTH YOUR SALT Season generously with salt and pepper before cooking for the flavors to better soak into the eggs.

BUTTER EFFECT We chose to cook the eggs in butter instead of olive or canola oil because it adds a milkiness to the dish, along with a cheesy, creamy taste that envelops the eggs.

CREAMY TEXTURE This dish doesn't rely on the color of the cooked eggs but rather a slow and precise coagulation. For runnier eggs, simply stir them gently while scraping the bottom of the pot with a wooden spoon or spatula. We don't recommend using a whisk at this stage because it can give the eggs a thin and homogeneous appearance.

TIME STARTS NOW Eggs continue to cook after they are removed from the heat, so we suggest removing them a bit early from the pan before they reach their desired final texture. Don't keep them warm before serving as they'll overcook.

French Omelet

PREPARATION 5 minutes
COOKING 3 minutes
SERVING 1

3	eggs
2 tsp	butter, softened, plus more for serving
	Finely chopped chives (optional)

Crack the eggs into a bowl. Season with salt and pepper. Whisk with a fork for 2 minutes or until smooth with no traces of egg white remaining.

In a small 8-inch (20 cm) non-stick skillet over medium-low heat, melt the butter without letting it brown.

Pour the eggs into the skillet and cook, stirring constantly with a spatula, until the mixture is starting to set, about 1 minute.

Once the eggs are almost dry but still creamy, reduce the heat to low. Tilt the skillet to slide the eggs to one side. Using the spatula, roll the omelet into a log. Tilt the skillet again, rolling the omelet onto a plate. The center of the omelet should still be very runny. Using a pastry brush, cover the omelet with butter and sprinkle with chives.

NUMBER OF INGREDIENTS You don't need to add water, milk or cream to this French classic; the eggs should remain the star of this dish. Simply add butter and then chives to garnish.

MIX LIGHTLY It's important that the omelet's texture is frothy and airy. To achieve this, mix the eggs with a fork until homogeneous, ensuring there are zero traces of white. Incorporate air into the eggs by whisking them up until the moment you pour the mixture into the skillet.

CHOOSE YOUR SKILLET Your choice of skillet plays an important role in cooking an omelet. Choose a small, non-stick version that will make rolling easy, along with a rubber spatula to avoid scratches. Before you cook the eggs, be sure to add butter to the skillet, letting it melt without browning—by coating the bottom of the skillet well, you'll keep the beaten eggs from sticking and scrambling.

PERFECTLY PALE The key to a good French omelet is gentle cooking as it risks drying out if cooked at a high temperature. Instead, turn on the burner to medium-low and wait for the skillet to get hot before pouring in the mixture. There should be no color on the surface of the omelet, only a light sheen from the butter.

Raspberry Scones

PREPARATION 30 minutes
COOKING 18 minutes per batch
MAKES 14
FREEZES WELL

Scones

¾ cup	(180 ml) milk
1	lemon, zest finely grated
2 tbsp	(30 ml) lemon juice
2¾ cups	(415 g) unbleached all-purpose flour
½ cup	(105 g) sugar
1½ tsp	baking powder
1 tsp	baking soda
¾ cup	(170 g) cold salted butter, diced
2 cups	(270 g) fresh or frozen raspberries

Topping

2 tbsp	salted butter, melted
2 tbsp	sugar

Scones

With the rack in the upper third, preheat the oven to 400°F (200°C). Line two baking sheets with silicone mats or parchment paper.

In a bowl, combine the milk, lemon zest and lemon juice. Let sit for 5 minutes.

In a food processor, combine the flour, sugar, baking powder and baking soda. Add the butter and pulse a few times, until it forms pea-sized pieces. Add the milk mixture and pulse just enough to moisten the dry ingredients. Do not overwork the dough.

On a floured work surface, using your fingers or a rolling pin, shape the dough into an 18-inch (45 cm) square. Cover with the raspberries. Loosely roll the dough up into a long log. Gently press the dough into a rectangle about 1¼ inches (3.5 cm) thick. Cut the dough into seven rectangles. Cut each rectangle in half to get two triangles. Place the scones on the baking sheets, evenly spaced out. Freeze at this point, if desired (see note).

Topping

Using a pastry brush, cover the scones with the melted butter. Sprinkle with the sugar. Bake one sheet at a time for 18 to 20 minutes or until the scones are golden. Let cool on a wire rack.

| NOTE | Once the raw scones are frozen, transfer them to an airtight container. They will keep for 3 months in the freezer. You can bake them from frozen by adding 5 minutes to the cooking time for a total of 23 to 25 minutes.

BETTER THAN BUTTERMILK Buttermilk is often used to help dough rise in the oven. After a few attempts, we decided instead on a mixture of milk and a good amount of lemon juice. This more acidic preparation helps the dough rise even more. And, bonus: these are basic ingredients you likely already have in your kitchen.

TRULY ALL-PURPOSE FLOUR We tried a version of this dough made with pastry flour, hoping to obtain a more crumbly and crisp dough. The result? The flour struggled to retain the fat and couldn't control the rise in the oven. All-purpose flour was therefore the best option. But be warned; to ensure a delicate dough, work it with your fingers as little as possible.

AN ABUNDANCE OF FRUIT Lemon is a popular flavor when it comes to scones, and its freshness pairs perfectly with butter. Here, we also include whole raspberries. Since you're only handling the dough gently with your fingers, when the raspberries are spread throughout it, they should remain almost intact. This means you'll get large pieces of fruit in each bite. Using smaller fruits like blueberries or blackberries is also a possibility.

BUTTER GLAZE We replaced buttermilk, which is normally brushed on the surface of the scones before baking, with melted unsalted butter. The scones brown even better and we then sprinkled on some sugar for a sparkling effect.

Ultra-Moist Banana Bread

PREPARATION 20 minutes
COOKING 1 hour
COOLING 1 hour
SERVINGS 8 to 10
FREEZES WELL

1½ cups	(225 g) unbleached all-purpose flour
1 tsp	baking powder
1 tsp	baking soda
1¼ cups	(310 ml) ripe bananas mashed with a fork (3 to 4 bananas)
½ cup	(125 ml) coconut milk (see note)
1 tbsp	(15 ml) lime juice
½ cup	(115 g) unsalted butter, softened
1 cup	(210 g) sugar
1	egg
1 tsp	(5 ml) vanilla

With the rack in the middle position, preheat the oven to 350°F (180°C). Butter a 9 × 5-inch (23 × 13 cm), 6-cup (1.5 L) loaf pan and line with a strip of parchment paper, letting it hang over two sides.

In a bowl, combine the flour, baking powder and baking soda. Set aside.

In another bowl, combine the mashed bananas with the coconut milk and lime juice.

In a third bowl, cream the butter and sugar with an electric mixer. Whisk in the egg and vanilla until smooth. With the machine running on low speed, stir in the dry ingredients, alternating with the banana mixture. Spread the batter out in the prepared pan.

Bake for 1 hour or until a toothpick inserted in the center of the bread comes out clean. Let cool on a wire rack for 1 hour before unmolding. On a work surface, slice the banana bread.

| NOTE | **Once a can of coconut milk has been opened, you can freeze any leftovers. If you don't have any coconut milk on hand, the coconut milk and lime juice can be replaced with ½ cup (125 ml) sour cream.**

COCONUT MILK FOR THE WIN Even though its taste is subtle, coconut milk provides an incomparable softness as well as the essential fat. Use regular, full-fat coconut milk over the light version, which won't yield the desired results.

THE KEY IS LIME Lime's tangy taste heightens the flavor of the banana in this recipe. It also helps develop the batter: when the lime reacts with the coconut milk, it mimics buttermilk by retaining humidity in the batter and keeping the cake moist longer.

GO BANANAS You want huge banana flavor for this recipe; all the more reason to add as many ripe bananas as possible! You don't want them completely black, just showing a few brown spots and feeling soft to the touch. 3 or 4 bananas (depending on their size) strike the right balance; if there are too many, the loaf won't be fully baked in the middle.

LEAVENING AGENT This loaf is extremely moist thanks to not only the coconut milk but also the baking soda. Baking soda, often used in cakes, ensures a good rise and brings softness to the crumb.

Crusty White Bread

PREPARATION 20 minutes
RISING 8 hours 45 minutes
COOKING 1 hour
MAKES 1 loaf, about 1⅔ lb (750 g)
FREEZES WELL

Dough

3½ cups	(525 g) unbleached all-purpose flour
1½ tsp	salt
½ tsp	instant yeast
1¾ cups	(430 ml) cold water

Coating

⅓ cup	(50 g) whole wheat flour

Dough

In a large Dutch oven or pot, combine the flour, salt and yeast. Add the water. Using a fork, stir until the flour is completely moistened but the dough is not entirely smooth. Cover and let rise for 8 to 12 hours or overnight at room temperature.

Coating

Place the whole wheat flour in a large bowl or directly on a work surface. Set aside.

With your hands, directly in the pot, deflate the dough by folding it onto itself about six times or until smooth.

Transfer the dough to the bowl (or to the work surface) and coat well with the whole wheat flour. Set aside. Clean out the pot.

Line the clean pot with parchment paper.

Place the dough at the center of the pot. Cover and let rise for 45 minutes at room temperature or until doubled in volume.

With the rack in the middle position, preheat the oven to 450°F (230°C).

Bake for 30 minutes. Remove the lid and continue to bake for 30 minutes.

Let the bread cool in the pot. Transfer the bread to a wire rack and let cool completely. Remove any excess flour.

FUSS-FREE BREAD Breadmaking takes time; this recipe requires a little patience, but takes only minimal handling. We chose to forgo kneading because it results in a beautiful honeycombed crumb.

FERMENTATION REWARD We use just a small amount of yeast to control its strong flavor from impacting the taste of the bread. Let the dough rise for a minimum of 8 hours to develop its intense aroma and allow the gluten to form.

BAKED TWICE During the first bake, the closed pot used in this recipe acts as a small oven filled with steam. It locks in moisture, which contributes to the development of a soft crumb and allows the bread to expand as much as possible. The rest of the baking takes place uncovered, allowing the crust to brown.

TYPE OF FLOUR There exist many types of bread made from various flours, but we use white all-purpose flour here for its versatility and availability. If you'd prefer another flour, we recommend replacing only up to a third of the amount required in the recipe. If you go beyond that proportion, the gluten will have trouble forming and the final result won't be the same.

RUSTIC CRUST There are many reasons to coat your dough with wheat flour. It helps regulate the baking and keeps the dough from sticking to the walls of the pot. And especially, it provides a nice, crusty texture that's reminiscent of a good country loaf.

Chocolate-Hazelnut Spread

PREPARATION 10 minutes
COOKING 5 minutes
CHILLING 2 hours
MAKES 2 cups (500 ml)
FREEZES WELL

1 cup	(250 ml) 35% cream
¼ cup	(55 g) sugar
3 tbsp	cocoa powder
6 oz	(170 g) milk chocolate, chopped
½ cup	(125 ml) hazelnut butter

In a small pot off the heat, whisk together the 35% cream, sugar and cocoa powder. Bring to a boil. Simmer for 1 minute while whisking.

Pour the mixture into a blender. Add the chocolate and hazelnut butter. Let melt for 1 minute. Purée the mixture until smooth. Watch out for splattering. Using a spatula, scrape down the sides of the blender as needed.

Pour the mixture into jars and let cool. Seal and refrigerate for 2 hours. Let sit out at room temperature before serving. The spread will keep for 2 to 3 weeks in the refrigerator or for 3 months in the freezer.

A TOUCH OF CHOCOLATE Store-bought chocolate hazelnut spreads typically rely on generous amounts of cocoa to bring the chocolaty taste. To achieve a nice smooth consistency with this homemade version, we reduce the amount of cocoa and add milk chocolate alongside.

ALL HAIL HAZELNUTS Along with chocolate, hazelnuts play a major role in this recipe. We tried using crushed whole hazelnuts, but with the equipment most people have at home, it would be hard to achieve the super-smooth texture required. We therefore settled on store-bought hazelnut butter. It may be harder to find and more expensive than other nut butters, but it makes all the difference.

WHISK IT GOOD This recipe doesn't contain any emulsifiers. That's why it's important, in the first step in the recipe, to whisk continuously for a full minute: this will ensure that the cocoa and sugar mix completely with the cream.

REFRIGERATION REQUIRED This spread has to be kept in the refrigerator because of the cream, which we chose over vegetable oil to get that velvety texture. If you can wait until the spread comes up to room temperature before you slather it on your toast, your patience will be rewarded!

Blueberry Muffins

PREPARATION 25 minutes
COOKING 20 minutes
MAKES 1 dozen
FREEZES WELL

1 cup	(250 ml) milk
1 tbsp	(15 ml) lemon juice
½ tsp	(2.5 ml) vanilla
1½ cups	(105 g) wheat bran cereal
1¼ cups	(190 g) unbleached all-purpose flour
1 tsp	baking powder
½ tsp	baking soda
¼ tsp	salt
2	eggs
¾ cup	(160 g) brown sugar
⅓ cup	(75 ml) vegetable oil
1½ cups	(225 g) fresh or frozen blueberries (see note)

With the rack in the middle position, preheat the oven to 350°F (180°C). Line a 12-cup muffin tin with silicone or paper liners.

In a bowl, combine the milk, lemon juice, vanilla and wheat bran. Let sit for 10 minutes or until the wheat bran is thoroughly soaked through.

In another bowl, combine the flour, baking powder, baking soda and salt.

In a third bowl, whisk together the eggs, brown sugar and oil. Add the wheat bran mixture and the dry ingredients. Using a spatula, mix just until the dry ingredients are moistened. Add the blueberries (set a few blueberries aside to garnish the muffins, if desired). Divide the batter among the muffin cups. Garnish with the reserved blueberries.

Bake for 20 to 25 minutes or until a toothpick inserted in the center of a muffin comes out clean. Let cool on a wire rack. The muffins will keep for 3 days, covered or in an airtight container, at room temperature.

| NOTE | **If you're using frozen blueberries, add them to the batter while still frozen at the very last minute. Otherwise, they will discolor the batter with an unappetizing result.**

LOADED WITH FRUIT For these muffins, we don't skimp on the amount of blueberries! We tested with both fresh and frozen options and both work beautifully. You could also use raspberries, cranberries or blackberries.

A TOUCH OF BUTTERMILK Many muffin recipes require yogurt to bring moisture to the batter. In this recipe, however, we use homemade buttermilk by combining lemon juice and milk. Soaking the whole-grain wheat bran cereal in the buttermilk and vanilla adds suppleness to the batter, all the while helping the muffins to rise.

SOFT BATTER Wheat bran cereal plays a large role in these muffins. Not only does it add fiber, making them more satiating, but also adds a desired softness. Once rehydrated and mixed in with the batter, it also adds moisture and provides a spongy texture, absorbing water without becoming soggy.

ULTRALIGHT We use vegetable oil rather than butter for these muffins for three reasons: Its flavor is neutral, letting the flavor of the blueberries shine through, the muffins end up lighter overall, and they can keep for longer.

Eggs Benedict

PREPARATION 40 minutes
COOKING 30 minutes
SERVINGS 4

Hollandaise Sauce

3 tbsp	(45 ml) water
1 tbsp	(15 ml) white wine vinegar
3	egg yolks
¾ cup	(170 g) unsalted butter, melted

Poached Eggs

1 tbsp	(15 ml) white vinegar
8	eggs

Toppings

8	slices Canadian back bacon or smoked ham
2 tbsp	butter
1 tsp	(5 ml) maple syrup
4	English muffins, halved
4	slices cooked crispy bacon, cut into small dice
1 tbsp	finely chopped chives

Hollandaise Sauce

In a bowl, whisk together the water, vinegar and egg yolks. Place the bowl over a pot of simmering water. Whisk until the texture becomes thick and frothy. Do not overcook the mixture so as not to scramble the egg yolks.

Remove the bowl from the pot. Off the heat, slowly drizzle in the melted butter, whisking constantly. Season with salt and pepper. Cover with plastic wrap directly on the surface of the sauce. Keep warm.

Poached Eggs

In a pot of simmering salted water, add the vinegar. Break the eggs one at a time into a small ramekin. Slide each egg into the simmering water. Poach 4 eggs at a time for about 3 minutes or until the desired doneness. The yolks should be runny. Using a slotted spoon, remove the eggs and drain them on a plate lined with paper towels.

Assembly

In a non-stick skillet over medium heat, cook the slices of back bacon in the butter and maple syrup for 1 minute or until warmed through. Set aside.

Toast the English muffins.

Spread some of the hollandaise sauce over each English muffin half. Top each muffin half with a slice of back bacon and a poached egg. Drizzle with the remaining sauce. Sprinkle with the chopped bacon and chives.

MAKE THE SAUCE For a rich and creamy hollandaise sauce, make sure that your water is just simmering rather than boiling when you place the egg yolks over the hot water bath. Whisk the yolks continuously; if you reach an omelet-like texture, it's because the water was too hot. There's no point in adding butter at this step if you haven't reached the desired consistency; it's best to simply start over.

VINEGAR OR LEMON? To emulsify the hollandaise sauce, some may prefer to use wine vinegar, while others opt for lemon juice. We like vinegar, because its taste marries well with that of the butter.

TASTY BACON We use back bacon here, rather than regular bacon. Its taste is reminiscent of ham, and its shape fits nicely with the English muffin. Warm it in butter with a touch of maple syrup to bring out its flavors.

THE FINAL TOUCH Make sure everything is served at the right temperature by keeping all the separate ingredients warm. You can also lightly warm the serving plates in the oven and toast the English muffins at the last moment. If your poached eggs cool, place them in hot water for just 30 seconds to reheat them. To keep your hollandaise sauce warm, set it in a bowl over the hot water bath used earlier, on an unlit stovetop burner.

Leek and Ham Quiche

PREPARATION 35 minutes
COOKING 1 hour 35 minutes
COOLING 2 hours 15 minutes
SERVINGS 10

Crust

1⅔ cups	(250 g) unbleached all-purpose flour
½ tsp	salt
½ cup	(115 g) cold unsalted butter, diced
⅓ cup	(75 ml) ice water
1	egg, lightly beaten

Filling

2½ cups	(240 g) thinly sliced leek (about 1 large leek)
2 tbsp	butter
6	eggs
2 cups	(500 ml) 15% cooking cream or half-and-half
½ lb	(225 g) white ham, diced
1¼ cups	(125 g) grated Gruyère cheese
½ tsp	salt
¼ tsp	ground nutmeg

Crust

In a food processor, blend the flour and salt. Add the butter and pulse a few times, until it forms pea-sized pieces. Add the water and egg. Pulse just until the dough starts coming together. Remove the dough from the food processor and shape into a disc with your hands. Cover with plastic wrap and refrigerate for 45 minutes.

On a floured work surface, roll the dough out to form a 15-inch (38 cm) circle. Using a pastry brush, remove any excess flour. Line an 8-inch (20 cm) springform pan with the dough. Let the dough hang over the sides of the pan. Prick the dough with a fork. Refrigerate for 45 minutes or freeze for 20 minutes.

With the rack in the lower third, preheat the oven to 400°F (200°C).

Remove the excess dough from around the side of the pan. Cover the dough with a piece of foil and fill with dried beans or ceramic pie weights. Place the pan on a baking sheet. Bake for 20 minutes or until the top edge of the crust is lightly browned. Carefully remove the pie weights and foil. Let the crust cool on a wire rack. Reduce the oven temperature to 325°F (165°C).

Filling

Meanwhile, in a large non-stick skillet over medium heat, cook the leek in the butter for 5 minutes or until softened. Season lightly with salt. Remove from the heat and let cool.

In a bowl, whisk the eggs. Add the 15% cream, three-quarters of the leek, and the ham, cheese, salt and nutmeg. Season with pepper. Pour into the cooled crust. Top with the remaining leek.

Bake for 1 hour 15 minutes or until the quiche is lightly browned and the center is just set. Let sit for 45 minutes before unmolding to allow the quiche to settle and set. Cut into wedges and serve.

BLIND BAKE Given that this quiche has a deep crust, blind baking is essential, which means partially baking the crust in the oven until it just starts to brown. The crust then won't absorb the moisture of the filling when it is added and, by the end of the quiche's baking time, the crust will be perfectly crisp.

STABLE CREAM To achieve a creamy yet light filling, use cooking cream with 15% fat. This cream is best to ensure stability during baking; it won't split, meaning it won't curdle or release water into the filling.

LOW COOKING TEMP To bake the quiche with the egg filling, reduce the oven's temperature to 325°F (165°C) so the crust doesn't brown too quickly. If the quiche starts to puff up and firm, stop baking immediately to prevent cracking and overcooking the eggs. Let it rest briefly so that the filling settles properly.

Baked Beans

PREPARATION 20 minutes
SOAKING 12 hours
COOKING 4 hours 35 minutes
WAITING 30 minutes
SERVINGS 6
FREEZES WELL

2¼ cups	(450 g) dried white beans or navy beans
1	piece (¾ lb/340 g) streaky salt pork with rind removed
1	large onion, chopped
2	garlic cloves, finely chopped
1 tbsp	butter
6 cups	(1.5 L) unsalted chicken broth
¼ cup	(60 ml) maple syrup
¼ cup	(60 ml) molasses
¼ cup	(60 ml) ketchup
2 tsp	dry mustard
½ tsp	ground black pepper
2	bay leaves

Place the beans in a large bowl. Cover with cold water and let soak for 12 hours or overnight at room temperature. Add water as needed, so the beans are always covered. Rinse and drain.

At the same time, place the salt pork in another bowl. Cover with cold water. Cover and refrigerate for 12 hours or overnight. Drain.

Place the salt pork in a small pot. Cover with cold water. Bring to a boil. Remove from the heat and let sit for 15 minutes. Drain. Set aside on a plate.

With the rack in the middle position, preheat the oven to 300°F (150°C).

In a Dutch oven over medium heat, brown the onion and garlic in the butter. Add the broth, maple syrup, molasses, ketchup, mustard, pepper and bay leaves as well as the white beans and salt pork. Mix well. Bring to a boil. Cover and transfer to the oven. Bake for 4 hours.

Remove from the oven and stir the beans. If the sauce is not thick enough, mash a few beans with the back of a wooden spoon. Cover and let rest for 15 minutes to let the sauce thicken. Adjust the seasoning.

Remove the salt pork and place on a work surface. Slice the pork, removing any excess fat as needed. Serve the beans with a slice of pork and toasted bread, if desired.

SWEET NOTES We prefer our baked beans less sweet, because excess sugar has the tendency to harden the beans, giving your mouth the impression that the beans are drier. A combination of equal parts molasses and maple syrup is, in our opinion, ideal. The distinctive fragrance of the latter helps to balance the more pronounced flavor of the molasses. If you like, you can add extra sweetness upon serving with a drizzle of syrup on your plate.

STRONG SOAK The salt pork is too salty to be used as is, and soaking it overnight alone just doesn't remove enough salt. The most efficient method is overnight soaking plus boiling the next day.

IN THE OVEN Beans baked in the oven develop a wonderful caramelized flavor, which is why we prefer this cooking method. When it comes to the cooking vessel, we preferred a cast-iron Dutch oven, good at sealing in steam to keep the beans from drying out. It's important to keep an eye on the liquid level as the beans cook to ensure it doesn't run low (the beans should always be covered).

BETTER THE NEXT DAY It's normal for the sauce to be runny when the cooking time is done, and it'll thicken as it cools. For this reason, we recommend waiting until the next day before eating the baked beans. They'll also taste even better once reheated, with the perfect texture and a well-balanced flavor.

Salmon Gravlax

PREPARATION 20 minutes
MARINATING 36 hours
SERVINGS 8

¼ cup	(60 g) coarse salt
¼ cup	(55 g) sugar
1	salmon fillet with skin, about 2½ lb (1.1 kg), taken from the thickest part of the fillet
2 tbsp	(30 ml) gin
½ cup	(20 g) dill, plus more for serving

In a bowl, combine the salt and sugar.

In a 13 × 9-inch (33 × 23 cm) glass dish, place the salmon skin-side down. Using a pastry brush, cover the salmon with the gin. Top with the salt mixture and dill. Cover with plastic wrap. Refrigerate for 36 hours.

Thoroughly rinse the salmon under cold running water. Pat very dry with paper towels.

On a work surface, using a very sharp knife, thinly slice the salmon flesh. Compost the skin.

Transfer the sliced gravlax to a serving dish. Garnish with dill fronds. Serve with toasted baguette slices, pumpernickel bread, sour cream and lemon wedges, if desired.

IRREPROACHABLE QUALITY The success of this Scandinavian dish relies on the freshness of the salmon. Make sure to mention to your fishmonger what you'll be using the salmon for, making sure it is firm, has a mild scent and is smooth and shiny.

SHEER SIMPLICITY Many versions exist, but we're sticking to the basics with this recipe: salmon, salt and sugar, with a touch of gin and dill. By in no way masking or altering the taste of the fish, we're highlighting its flavor by showcasing it in its purest form.

WORTH THE WAIT Given that it takes 2 days to prepare, gravlax isn't a last-minute decision; it's one you prepare and wait for before you can enjoy it. A curing time of 36 hours is needed to infuse the salmon with flavor. By ridding the fish of its water content, the salt changes its texture, making it very moist.

SLICE THINLY For beautifully thin slices, we recommend first cutting the fillet into three equal pieces and then slicing thinly against the grain. This allows for better control over the size of your slices, more precision and a nice texture.

The Best
Main Dishes

Meatballs in Tomato Sauce

PREPARATION 35 minutes
COOKING 55 minutes
SERVINGS 6
FREEZES WELL

Tomato Sauce

3	garlic cloves, chopped
1	bay leaf
¼ tsp	red pepper flakes
2 tbsp	(30 ml) olive oil
1 can	(28 oz/796 ml) whole plum tomatoes

Meatballs

2	slices white sandwich bread
¼ cup	(60 ml) milk
1 lb	(450 g) ground veal
2 cups	(140 g) finely grated fresh Parmesan cheese
1	egg
1	garlic clove, finely chopped
¼ cup	(10 g) finely chopped flat-leaf parsley
½ tsp	salt
½ tsp	ground fennel seeds
¼ tsp	dried oregano
¼ tsp	red pepper flakes

Tomato Sauce

In a large non-stick skillet over medium-high heat, lightly brown the garlic, bay leaf and red pepper flakes in the oil. Add the tomatoes and simmer over low heat for 30 minutes or until they are starting to burst. Using a potato masher, coarsely crush the tomatoes. Season with salt and pepper. Keep warm.

Meatballs

Meanwhile, in a food processor, pulse the bread into breadcrumbs. In a large bowl, soak the breadcrumbs in the milk for 5 minutes. Add the veal, Parmesan, egg, garlic, parsley, salt, fennel seeds, oregano and red pepper flakes and mix well with your hands.

With lightly oiled hands, shape the meat mixture into meatballs using about 2 tbsp for each one.

Place the meatballs in the tomato sauce. Cover and cook over medium-low heat for 10 minutes, turning them over a few times during cooking.

Remove the lid and continue to cook for 10 minutes or until the meatballs are cooked through. Remove and compost the bay leaf.

Serve the meatballs and sauce with blanched rapini, if desired.

ALL ABOUT VEAL After testing a combination of pork, beef and veal, we found that veal alone makes for the most tender meatballs, given that it contains the most gelatin. To maintain the delicate texture of the meat, it's best to mix it using your hands rather than with a stand mixer.

PECORINO OR PARMESAN? Instead of Pecorino, we use fresh Parmesan because it has less salt and a mild taste. As a general rule, we recommend a 1:3 cheese-to-meat ratio. Using more cheese overpowers the taste of the other ingredients. Finely grated cheese that looks like snow will ensure your meatballs have a uniform texture. Ask your cheesemonger to do it for you or get out your microplane and grate away.

SLICED BREAD Fresh bread soaked in milk gives us the texture we are looking for here. We preferred ordinary sliced white sandwich bread for perfectly moist meatballs, as opposed to whole wheat bread, which dried them out during testing.

COOK IN THE SAUCE We do not brown our meatballs because it dries them out. Meatballs that simmer directly in the sauce, however, are so soft you can cut them with a spoon. Bonus: The tomato sauce infuses the meatballs with flavorful acidity and umami.

Meat Lasagna

PREPARATION 45 minutes
COOKING 2 hours 30 minutes
WAITING 15 minutes
SERVINGS 8
FREEZES WELL

Meat Sauce

1½ tsp	pickling spice
½ tsp	fennel seeds
¼ tsp	red pepper flakes
¾ lb	(340 g) lean ground pork
¾ lb	(340 g) lean ground beef
3 tbsp	(45 ml) olive oil
2	onions, chopped
2	celery stalks, chopped
3	garlic cloves, finely chopped
2 cans	(28 oz/796 ml each) whole plum tomatoes
1 tsp	dried oregano

Béchamel Sauce

3 tbsp	butter
¼ cup	(40 g) unbleached all-purpose flour
2½ cups	(625 ml) milk
½ cup	(35 g) finely grated fresh Parmesan cheese

Lasagna

12	lasagna noodles
4 cups	(400 g) grated caciocavallo or mozzarella cheese
1 tbsp	finely chopped flat-leaf parsley
1 tbsp	finely chopped chives

Meat Sauce

Using a mortar and pestle or spice grinder, blend the pickling spice, fennel seeds and red pepper flakes into a powder.

In a large pot over high heat, cook the pork and beef with the ground spices in the oil, breaking the meat up with a wooden spoon until golden. Season with salt and pepper. Add the onions, celery and garlic. Cook over medium heat for another 5 minutes.

Add the tomatoes and oregano to the pot. Using a potato masher, purée the tomatoes. Bring the sauce to a boil. Simmer gently for 1 hour 30 minutes, stirring often, until the sauce has reduced by one-quarter. Adjust the seasoning.

Béchamel Sauce

Meanwhile, in a pot over medium heat, melt the butter. Add the flour and cook for 1 minute while whisking. Whisk in the milk. Bring to a boil while whisking. Simmer gently for 2 minutes or until the sauce thickens. Stir in the Parmesan. Season with salt and pepper. Cover and keep warm.

Lasagna

Meanwhile, in a large pot of boiling salted water, cook the lasagna noodles until very al dente. Drain. Coat the noodles with oil and spread out on a baking sheet. Cover with a damp kitchen towel or plastic wrap.

With the rack in the middle position, preheat the oven to 375°F (190°C).

Assembly

Cover the bottom of a 13 × 9-inch (33 × 23 cm) baking dish with ½ cup (125 ml) of the hot meat sauce. Cover with a layer of noodles.

Top the noodles with 2 cups (500 ml) of the meat sauce and ⅔ cup (150 ml) of the béchamel. Sprinkle with ⅔ cup (65 g) of the grated caciocavallo cheese. Cover with another layer of noodles.

Repeat the previous step, layering in the ingredients in the same order. Finish off with a layer of noodles, the remaining meat sauce and grated cheese (you can freeze the lasagna at this stage without the cheese, if desired). Place the dish on a baking sheet. Bake for 25 minutes.

Remove the lasagna from the oven. In a small bowl, combine the parsley and chives. Sprinkle over the lasagna. Continue to bake for 10 minutes or until the cheese is golden. Let sit for 15 minutes before serving.

ESSENTIAL BÉCHAMEL By spreading béchamel sauce between the pasta and sauce layers, we're adding richness and creaminess to this lasagna. The béchamel marries perfectly with the abundance of meat sauce, and reduces its acidity slightly, making the taste richer and smoother overall. As the béchamel contains a good dose of Parmesan cheese, there's no need to add it between the pasta layers also.

CHEESE CHANGES EVERYTHING For a lasagna to stand out, the choice of cheese is essential. From all the options we tested, we selected caciocavallo, a firm cheese that becomes very runny and melts when heated, and that has a pleasant creamy taste.

STUNNING SPICES Accentuate the flavors of the meat by seasoning it with pickling spice. Surprising, we know! This spice consists of coriander, mustard, caraway, black pepper, allspice and bay leaves, which pair wonderfully with the sauce.

NECESSARY REST The resting time after cooking isn't just a suggestion. These few minutes allow the lasagna to settle so that it holds together well, and when it's time to cut it, you get beautiful pieces that don't fall apart on the plate.

Bolognese Sauce

PREPARATION 30 minutes
COOKING 2 hours
MAKES 6 cups (1.5 L)
FREEZES WELL

1	onion, chopped
1	celery stalk, chopped
2	carrots, chopped
2	garlic cloves, chopped
4 oz	(115 g) mild pancetta, cut into small pieces
1 oz	(30 g) mortadella, cut into small pieces
2 tbsp	butter
1 lb	(450 g) medium-lean ground beef
½ lb	(225 g) lean ground veal
½ lb	(225 g) lean ground pork
½ cup	(125 ml) red wine
⅓ cup	(75 ml) tomato paste
2 cups	(500 ml) chicken broth
2 tsp	mixed finely chopped herb leaves (such as sage, marjoram, thyme)
2	bay leaves
1 pinch	red pepper flakes
½ cup	(125 ml) milk

In a food processor, finely chop the onion, celery, carrots and garlic. Set aside on a plate.

In the food processor, finely chop the pancetta and mortadella.

In a pot over high heat, soften the vegetables in the butter for 5 minutes. Season with salt and pepper. Add the pancetta, mortadella, ground beef, ground veal and ground pork. Cook the meat, breaking it up with a wooden spoon and stirring occasionally, until the cooking juices have evaporated and the meat is nicely browned.

Deglaze with the wine and let reduce until almost dry. Add the tomato paste and cook for 1 minute while stirring. Add the broth, chopped herb leaves, bay leaves and red pepper flakes. Mix well. Cover and simmer over medium-low heat for 1 hour, stirring occasionally.

Remove the lid. Add the milk and continue to cook, uncovered, for 30 minutes, stirring occasionally. Adjust the seasoning.

BEGIN WITH *BATTUTO* Standard in many Italian dishes, *battuto* is what we use to get this ragù rolling. Like a French mirepoix, it's a mixture of finely chopped onions, carrots, celery and garlic. You want to mince the ingredients as finely as possible, so a food processor helps. Use yours to finely chop the pancetta and mortadella, too, which you add to the veggie medley.

DAIRY PRODUCTS Some Italians like butter—a lot. In northern Italy, dairy is common and butter is used as liberally as olive oil is in the southern parts of the country. For our ragù, we use butter and milk: the butter to round out our battuto and to coat the pasta before adding our sauce, and the milk to balance the acid from the tomato paste and bind the sauce.

THREE MEATS Although some ragùs call for chicken livers, we like the combination of ground beef, pork and veal: beef to give a deep, meaty flavor, pork for fat and full body, and veal to add a more delicate dimension.

OTHER INGREDIENTS For the perfect balance, add just a bit of tomato paste to give a deep, dark color to the sauce, and a touch of umami. Red wine (which can be replaced with white) and broth both bring flavor and richness to the dish.

Pasta Carbonara

PREPARATION 15 minutes
COOKING 15 minutes
SERVINGS 2

¼ lb	(115 g) pancetta, diced
1 tbsp	(15 ml) olive oil
1 tsp	black peppercorns, crushed
½ lb	(225 g) spaghettoni
4	egg yolks
¾ cup	(75 g) finely grated fresh Parmesan cheese
¾ cup	(75 g) finely grated fresh Pecorino cheese

In a large skillet over medium-high heat, brown the pancetta in the oil. Add the crushed pepper and continue to cook for 1 minute while stirring. Set the pancetta aside on a plate, leaving the cooking fat in the skillet.

In a pot of lightly salted boiling water, cook the pasta until very al dente. Set aside 1½ cups (375 ml) of the cooking water. Drain the pasta.

In a bowl, combine the egg yolks with the Parmesan and Pecorino and ¼ cup (60 ml) of the reserved pasta water. Set aside.

In the skillet with the pancetta cooking fat, continue to cook the pasta with ½ cup (125 ml) of the pasta water, stirring constantly, until al dente and the liquid has evaporated. Add more pasta water if it evaporates before the pasta has fully finished cooking. Remove from the heat.

Add the egg yolk mixture and pancetta to the pasta. Return the skillet to medium heat to thicken the sauce slightly, stirring the pasta constantly to prevent the eggs from coagulating. Add more pasta water to thin out the sauce as needed. Adjust the seasoning.

Divide the pasta between two shallow bowls. Season generously with pepper. Serve immediately.

COOKING WATER Once you've boiled your pasta, the water will be rich in starch. Use a small amount to finish up the dish in the skillet; add it to the egg and cheese mixture, and it'll bind and add creaminess to the sauce.

CLASSIC CHEESES We do as the Romans do and use both Pecorino and Parmesan in the sauce. The former is a salty, hard-rind cheese made from sheep's milk that helps enhance the flavor of the mixture. As for the latter, we prefer not to grate it over the dish upon serving, but add it directly to the sauce instead, making it smooth and creamy when melted.

MEAL FOR TWO This recipe yields two servings. Given that the pasta absorbs the liquid pretty quickly, it will cook unevenly if the skillet is overcrowded. This means there won't be enough sauce for additional servings, even if you increase the ingredients. Instead, if you want to make this dish for four, both double the ingredients and cook it simultaneously in two separate skillets.

CREAMY YOLKS Instead of including the egg whites, which coagulate quickly and tend to make the sauce grainy, we use the yolks only. These make the dish creamy, rich and tasty, and are the reason the recipe doesn't require any cream.

PLUMP NOODLES For this recipe, we went with spaghettoni, not to be confused with spaghettini. These noodles are more plump than regular spaghetti, and are easier to work into the sauce.

Mushroom Risotto

PREPARATION 25 minutes
COOKING 40 minutes
SERVINGS 4

½ oz	(14 g) dried bolete (or porcini) mushrooms
8 cups	(2 L) chicken broth
1½ lb	(675 g) white mushrooms, coarsely chopped
2	garlic cloves, chopped
¼ cup	(55 g) butter
2	shallots, chopped
2 cups	(420 g) arborio rice
¾ cup	(180 ml) dry white wine
1½ cups	(105 g) grated fresh Parmesan cheese, plus more for serving

In a small bowl of water, quickly rinse the dried mushrooms to remove any sand. Using a slotted spoon, remove the mushrooms from the water. Discard the water. On a work surface, coarsely chop the dried mushrooms. Place in a pot with the broth. Bring to a boil and keep warm.

Meanwhile, in a large skillet over medium-high heat, cook the white mushrooms and garlic in 3 tbsp of the butter until the water released from the mushrooms has completely evaporated and they are starting to brown. Add more butter as needed.

In a large pot, soften the shallots in the remaining butter. Add the rice and cook for 1 minute, stirring to coat the grains with the butter. Add the wine and let reduce until almost dry, stirring constantly. Add the browned mushrooms.

Over medium heat, add the broth (with the dried mushrooms) to the pot of rice, about 1 cup (250 ml) at a time, stirring often until the liquid is completely absorbed before adding more broth. Season with salt and pepper. Cook for 18 to 20 minutes or until the rice is al dente and the risotto is slightly runny but the broth has thickened. Remove from the heat and let sit for 2 minutes. Add the Parmesan and stir vigorously for 30 seconds. Adjust the seasoning.

Serve the risotto in shallow bowls. It should spread out in the bowl, leaving a small mound at the center. Garnish with more Parmesan. Serve immediately.

ABUNDANT MUSHROOMS You want this risotto to be bursting with mushroom flavor! To achieve this, infuse the dried boletes or porcini directly in the chicken broth. We use these varieties for their woodsy, more pronounced flavor. We also include a large amount (three containers!) of white mushrooms, chopped with garlic, and we continue to cook those along with the rice.

THE RIGHT RICE Arborio rice is the ultimate choice when cooking risotto. It brings richness and creaminess, and absorbs flavors easily. We recommend not rinsing arborio rice, as its starch content is key to the characteristic creaminess of risotto. Avoid varieties of rice referred to as "risotto rice," because these don't hold up as well to cooking.

ONE LADLE AT A TIME To achieve the best risotto, it's important to add only one ladle of broth at a time to the rice as it cooks. This way, you have more control over the broth's absorption and evaporation. Adding liquid only when the level is low also yields a creamier texture. It's possible you might not need the entire amount of liquid called for in the recipe.

TRUE TEXTURE A true risotto should have a creamy, almost fluid texture. When ladled into a bowl, it shouldn't form a dense ball, but rather spread out in the dish. The Italian term is all'onda, meaning it should form a wave when you gently shake the pot.

Pizza Dough

PREPARATION 15 minutes
RISING 2 hours
MAKES 2 pizzas, 11 inches (28 cm) each
FREEZES WELL

2⅔ cups	(400 g) unbleached all-purpose flour
2 tsp	sugar
1 tsp	instant yeast
1 tsp	salt
1¼ cups	(310 ml) warm water

In a large bowl, using a wooden spoon, combine the flour, sugar, yeast and salt. Add the water and stir until smooth, about 2 minutes. Cover with plastic wrap and let rise in a warm, humid spot for 1 hour or until doubled in volume.

On a lightly floured work surface, knead the dough for 2 minutes. Cut the dough into two equal pieces. Shape each piece into a ball and place in a large airtight container or on a lightly floured baking sheet. Cover with plastic wrap (see note). Let rise for 1 hour or until doubled in volume.

| NOTE | You can refrigerate the balls of dough at this point for up to 48 hours. Let sit out at room temperature for 1 hour before using. You can also freeze the dough at this point. Once frozen, cover each ball of dough with plastic wrap and transfer to an airtight container. When ready to use, thaw out in the refrigerator. Once thawed, let sit in a warm, humid spot for 1 hour.

To cook your homemade pizzas in a pizza oven:

Preheat the pizza oven on high (MAX) with the door closed for 20 minutes.

Do not use parchment paper. Instead, place the rolled-out dough on a lightly floured pizza peel before covering with toppings. Using the pizza peel, slide the pizza onto the hot stone. Bake in the pizza oven for 2 to 3 minutes, or until the crust is golden, rotating the pizza 4 or 5 times during cooking.

For the Margherita Pizza (p. 89), bake it in two stages, as indicated in the recipe, for 1 to 2 minutes each time.

SUGAR AND SALT As with any pizza dough, this recipe is a fundamental balance between flour, water and yeast, but the sugar and salt play important roles too. Sugar and water both influence the pizza's flavor and texture; sugar also helps the yeast do its job and contributes to the dough's caramelization in the oven. Salt, meanwhile, helps form a crisp crust as it bakes.

THE IMPORTANCE OF WATER Pizza dough is expected to have a good moisture content, allowing it to develop gluten and elasticity, which is why the amount of water is important. Don't worry if the dough looks a bit liquidy; as it rises the first time, the water will hydrate the flour, allowing the gluten to form.

LET IT REST Each step contributes to the success of a delicious pizza dough. As you knead it, the dough gains strength and structure, becoming smooth and homogeneous. After shaping the dough into a ball and letting it rise a second time, it loses that excess elasticity and keeps its shape when rolled out.

CHILL YOUR DOUGH If you're not using it right away, the ball of dough can be refrigerated for up to 48 hours, or frozen. Chilling the dough not only makes it easier to handle later, but also enhances its flavor.

Margherita Pizza

PREPARATION 30 minutes
COOKING 45 minutes
MAKES 2 pizzas, 11 inches (28 cm) each
SAUCE FREEZES WELL

Sauce

1	small garlic clove, finely chopped
⅛ tsp	red pepper flakes
1 tbsp	(15 ml) olive oil, plus more for serving
1 can	(28 oz/796 ml) whole San Marzano plum tomatoes
1 tsp	salt

Pizzas

1	recipe Pizza Dough (p. 87)
2 tbsp	finely grated fresh Pecorino cheese
6	basil leaves, plus more for serving
1 ball	(200 g) fresh cow's milk mozzarella (fior di latte), drained and coarsely chopped
	Fleur de sel (optional)

Sauce

In a small pot over medium heat, soften the garlic with the red pepper flakes in the oil for 30 seconds. Add the tomatoes and salt. Using a potato masher, purée the tomatoes. Bring to a boil.

Simmer over low heat, stirring occasionally, for 15 to 20 minutes or until the sauce thickens. Remove from the heat and let cool. Transfer to an airtight container and refrigerate until ready to use. The sauce will keep for 5 days in the refrigerator or for 3 months in the freezer.

Pizzas

Meanwhile, place a pizza stone on the middle rack of the oven. Preheat the oven to 500°F (260°C) for 45 minutes (see p. 87 for pizza oven cooking instructions).

On a generously floured work surface, working with one ball of pizza dough at a time, press with your hands to form an 11-inch (28 cm) circle, keeping a thick border all the way around.

Remove any excess flour. Place the dough on a piece of parchment paper. Cover with ¼ cup (60 ml) of the tomato sauce. Sprinkle with half of the Pecorino (1 tbsp).

Using a pizza peel or inverted baking sheet, slide one pizza at a time with the parchment paper onto the hot pizza stone. Bake for 4 minutes.

Remove the pizza from the oven. Remove the parchment paper. Top the pizza with 3 basil leaves and half of the mozzarella. Continue to bake for 4 to 5 minutes or until the crust is golden.

Once out of the oven, top the pizza with a pinch of fleur de sel. Drizzle with olive oil and garnish with a few more basil leaves. Cut into wedges and serve immediately.

TOMATO SAUCE The choice of tomatoes is crucial to a good sauce. San Marzano are a good option, because they're very sweet and break down easily, but you can also go with another good-quality whole plum tomato. Reducing the sauce concentrates its flavor and gets rid of excess water that would otherwise make the dough soggy.

HIGH HEAT To make a great pizza, you need a very hot oven. You want the crust to get crispy and brown quickly while staying soft on the inside. If you don't own a pizza oven, a pizza stone also yields good results.

TWICE THE CHEESE We use two types of cheese added at two different points during cooking. Pecorino brings depth and umami as it binds to the sauce, further flavoring it with its salty side. Mozzarella goes on top of the pizza in small pieces before a short stint in the oven, adding stretch and a touch of milkiness.

SIMPLE TOPPINGS With its tomato sauce, cheeses, fleur de sel and a drizzle of olive oil, along with a few basil leaves, this pizza's toppings are few. But we love the Margherita precisely for its simplicity, its balanced seasoning and the soft texture of its dough.

Mushroom Pizza

PREPARATION 50 minutes
COOKING 30 minutes
MAKES 2 pizzas, 11 inches (28 cm) each
FREEZES WELL

¼ oz	(7 g) dried bolete (or porcini) mushrooms (optional)
1 lb	(450 g) white mushrooms, thinly sliced
1	garlic clove, chopped
3 tbsp	butter
¼ cup	(60 ml) dry white wine
1	recipe Pizza Dough (p. 87)
⅔ cup	(150 ml) crème fraîche (see note)
2 tbsp	finely grated fresh Parmesan cheese, plus more for serving
2	shallots, thinly sliced
1 ball	(100 g) buffalo mozzarella, drained and torn into pieces

Place a pizza stone on the middle rack of the oven. Preheat the oven to 500°F (260°C) for 45 minutes (see p. 87 for pizza oven cooking instructions).

Meanwhile, in a small bowl of water, quickly rinse the dried mushrooms to remove any sand. Using a slotted spoon, remove the mushrooms from the water. Discard the water. On a work surface, coarsely chop the dried mushrooms.

In a large skillet over medium-high heat, cook the white mushrooms and garlic in the butter until the water released from the mushrooms has completely evaporated and they are starting to brown. Add more butter as needed. Add the dried mushrooms and wine. Let reduce until dry. Season with salt and pepper. Remove from the heat.

On a generously floured work surface, working with one ball of pizza dough at a time, press with your hands into an 11-inch (28 cm) circle, keeping a thick border all the way around. Remove any excess flour. Place the dough on a piece of parchment paper. Top with half of the crème fraîche (⅓ cup/75 ml), half of the Parmesan (1 tbsp), half of the shallots and half of the mozzarella. Season with salt and pepper. Garnish with half of the mushrooms.

Using a pizza peel or inverted baking sheet, slide one pizza at a time with the parchment paper onto the hot pizza stone. Bake for 8 minutes or until the crust is golden.

Once out of the oven, sprinkle with a little more Parmesan. Cut into wedges and serve immediately.

| NOTE | **Crème fraîche can sometimes be difficult to find. If it's not available, combine ⅓ cup (75 ml) 35% cream with ⅓ cup (75 ml) sour cream.**

PROFUSION OF MUSHROOMS These pizzas are loaded with a generous amount of mushrooms; about one container each. You can use simply white mushrooms, but the strong taste of the dried boletes or porcini definitely takes the pizza to a whole other level.

Browning the mushrooms in a skillet intensifies their flavor.

WHITE SAUCE To highlight the mushrooms, we use a creamy white sauce, made simply with crème fraîche and grated Parmesan cheese.

THE POWER OF SHALLOTS Before sliding the pizza into the oven, add raw, thinly sliced shallots on top. Without them, the pizza will be a bit bland, but when they're added, they strongly flavor the cream in a way that's reminiscent of an Alsatian pizza.

VERY HOT OVEN To keep the dough from drying out as it cooks, make sure your oven is very hot (500°F/260°C). This allows the dough to brown while the inside stays soft. This recipe is the perfect opportunity to use your oven's convection mode or, even better, to use a pizza oven.

Spaghetti Sauce

PREPARATION 40 minutes
COOKING 3 hours 45 minutes
MAKES 20 cups (5 L)
FREEZES WELL

1½ lb	(675 g) mild or spicy Italian sausage meat (ideally a mixture of both)
1½ lb	(675 g) lean ground beef
¼ to ½ tsp	red pepper flakes
¼ cup	(60 ml) olive oil
3	onions, finely chopped
4	carrots, diced
4	celery stalks, diced
4	garlic cloves, finely chopped
1 can	(5½ oz/156 ml) tomato paste
2 cans	(28 oz/796 ml each) diced plum tomatoes
2 cans	(28 oz/796 ml each) tomato sauce or crushed tomatoes in purée
2 cups	(500 ml) beef broth
2 tsp	dried oregano
2 to 3	cloves

In a large pot over medium-high heat, cook the sausage meat with half of the red pepper flakes in 1 tbsp (15 ml) of the oil, breaking the meat up with a wooden spoon until golden, adding more oil as needed. Season the meat with salt and pepper and set aside in a bowl. Repeat with the ground beef, remaining red pepper flakes and 1 tbsp (15 ml) of the oil, cooking until nicely browned. Season with salt and pepper and set aside in a bowl.

In the same pot, soften the onions, carrots, celery and garlic in the remaining oil. Season with salt and pepper. Add the tomato paste and continue to cook for 1 minute while stirring.

Return all of the meat to the pot. Add the tomatoes, tomato sauce, broth, oregano and cloves. Mix well. Bring to a boil. Simmer gently for 3 hours, stirring often and scraping the bottom of the pot, just until the sauce thickens. Remove the cloves before serving. Serve over pasta.

The sauce will keep for 5 days in the refrigerator.

CHOICE OF MEAT A true spaghetti sauce needs meat! We began our tests with a combination of pork, veal and beef. While it was interesting, the flavor was less classic. We ultimately decided on a mix of equal parts ground beef and Italian sausages, both mild and spicy, for a lovely balance of flavors.

VEGETABLE TRIO The classic trio of carrot, celery and garlic are the aromatic base of the sauce here. We purposely omitted green peppers, as their pronounced flavor masks that of the other ingredients. If you enjoy mushrooms, you can add them here. Two or three 8 oz (225 g) containers of finely chopped mushrooms will yield a texture similar to that of meat. You can even replace part of the meat with mushrooms.

A TOUCH OF AROMATICS When it comes to choosing aromatics, we limited ourselves to oregano (essential in a tomato sauce!) and cloves, which are not dominant here and only provide fragrance. We steer clear of prepared Italian herb blends, as their flavor can sometimes be overpowering.

TOTALLY TOMATO Begin with tomato paste, which brings a nice concentration of flavors. For the canned diced tomatoes, go for an Italian variety, especially San Marzano; they're on the pricier end, but truly delicious. Also add tomato sauce for a smooth and velvety texture—homemade is best, otherwise plain store-bought will work just fine.

Oven-Roasted Barbecue Chicken

PREPARATION 35 minutes
MARINATING 2 days
COOKING 1 hour 15 minutes
SERVINGS 4

Chicken

1	chicken, about 3 lb (1.4 kg)
1 tsp	salt

Barbecue Seasoning

2 tbsp	(30 ml) ketchup
2 tbsp	butter, softened
2 tsp	sweet paprika
2 tsp	dry mustard
1 tsp	brown sugar
½ tsp	onion powder
½ tsp	garlic powder
½ tsp	ground black pepper
¼ tsp	celery salt

Barbecue Sauce

2 tbsp	butter
2 tbsp	unbleached all-purpose flour
2	garlic cloves, chopped
2 cans	(10 oz/284 ml each) condensed chicken broth, undiluted
1 tbsp	(15 ml) ketchup
2 tsp	sweet paprika
1 tsp	dry mustard
1 tsp	(5 ml) honey
¼ tsp	ground ginger
1 pinch	cayenne pepper
1 pinch	ground nutmeg

Chicken

In a large glass baking dish, arrange the chicken, breast-side up. Sprinkle the entire surface of the chicken with the salt, focusing primarily on the legs and breasts. Cover with plastic wrap and refrigerate for 2 days.

Barbecue Seasoning

With the rack in the middle position, preheat the oven to 375°F (190°C).

In a bowl, combine the ketchup and butter.

On a work surface, using your fingers, gently detach the skin from the breast and legs of the chicken, being careful not to tear the skin. Spread the butter mixture between the meat and skin.

In another bowl, combine the paprika, mustard, brown sugar, onion powder, garlic powder, pepper and celery salt. Sprinkle the spice mixture over the entire surface of the chicken. Return to the baking dish.

Bake, uncovered, for 1 hour 15 minutes or until a thermometer inserted in the thigh without touching bone reads 180°F (82°C). Using a pastry brush, baste the chicken with the cooking juices halfway through cooking.

Barbecue Sauce

Meanwhile, in a pot over medium heat, melt the butter. Add the flour and garlic. Cook for 2 minutes, whisking, until the mixture is golden. Add the broth. Bring to a boil while whisking. Add the ketchup, paprika, mustard, honey, ginger, cayenne and nutmeg. Simmer for 10 minutes or until the sauce thickens. The sauce will keep for 5 days in an airtight container in the refrigerator. When ready to serve, reheat the sauce. Add some broth to thin out the sauce as needed.

Serve the chicken and barbecue sauce with Homemade Fries (p. 15), if desired.

DRY BRINE This technique is often used on turkey, but it works just as well with chicken. The dry brine is a practical method that allows the meat to retain moisture and the salt to permeate the meat.

BARBECUE SPICES A good BBQ chicken needs some kick! The brown sugar in the spice blend adds caramelization and also helps cut the bitterness of the oven-roasted spices. Garlic and onion powders are necessary, as they provide flavor reminiscent of store-bought roast chicken. The blend of butter and ketchup rubbed underneath the skin adds sweetness and gives the impression that the chicken is even juicier.

RIGHT HEAT For juicy meat and crispy skin, you need a hot 375°F (190°C) oven. We found that starting at a high temperature and then gradually decreasing it, as many recipes suggest, didn't really give us any better results.

CONCENTRATED SAUCE The brown roux base (cooked butter and flour used to bind the sauce) adds a caramelized flavor to the sauce and toasts the garlic at the same time. As for the well-balanced spice blend, it adds a complexity of flavor.

Maple-Braised Ham

PREPARATION 15 minutes
COOKING 4 hours
WAITING 15 minutes
SERVINGS 8
FREEZES WELL

1	bone-in smoked pork shoulder (picnic ham), about 4½ lb (2 kg)
1 cup	(250 ml) amber maple syrup
1	onion, halved
1 tsp	black peppercorns

Remove the string from the ham. Place the ham in a large pot and cover with cold water. Bring to a boil. Simmer over medium heat for 30 minutes. Remove the ham from the pot and discard the water.

Return the ham to the pot. Add the maple syrup, onion and peppercorns and cover with cold water. Bring to a boil. Cover and simmer gently for 3 hours or until the meat easily falls from the bone, turning the pork over halfway through cooking. Add water as needed. Remove from the heat. Let sit for 15 minutes.

Remove the ham from the pot and place on a work surface. Remove and compost the rind. Debone the ham and remove any excess fat. Strain the broth through a sieve set over a large measuring cup or bowl. Compost the aromatics.

On a serving dish, arrange the pieces of ham and drizzle with some of the hot broth. Serve with Mashed Potatoes (p. 43) and vegetables, if desired.

PICNIC HAM We chose bone-in pork shoulder, also known as picnic ham. It's fattier and tastier than both the ham butt and toupie-style ham. As for the bone, it's essential; ham cooked with the bone is more flavorful than one cooked without. The bone also helps monitor the doneness: if you're able to turn the bone easily in the meat, the ham is perfectly heated through.

WITH THE RIND Fat means flavor, so it's best to keep the skin on when cooking your ham. It also acts as a protective layer, preventing the meat inside from drying out. Once cooked, the skin can be easily peeled off.

DESALTING Ham is a rather salty piece of meat. Before braising, make sure to remove excess salt by simmering the meat in boiling water for 30 minutes. Taste the water and if it's salty, replace it and continue cooking. We also recommend removing the netting that surrounds the ham upon purchase, or the fat and meat will stick to it as it cooks.

AMBER MAPLE SYRUP We prefer amber maple syrup over golden for its more robust flavor. Save the sweet and savory broth at the end to drizzle over the meat before serving, or use it as a base for cooking potatoes.

Chicken Pot Pie

PREPARATION 55 minutes
CHILLING 1 hour
COOKING 1 hour 20 minutes
WAITING 45 minutes
SERVINGS 6
FREEZES WELL

Shortcrust Pastry

1	egg, separated
1 cup	(250 ml) cold water
1 tbsp	(15 ml) white vinegar
4⅓ cups	(650 g) unbleached all-purpose flour
1 tsp	salt
1 lb	(450 g) cold vegetable shortening, cubed

Béchamel

⅓ cup	(75 g) unsalted butter
6 tbsp	(60 g) unbleached all-purpose flour
3	green onions, chopped
1½ cups	(375 ml) chicken broth
1 cup	(250 ml) milk, plus more for brushing

Filling

1 cup	(145 g) diced carrots (about 1 large carrot)
½ cup	(75 g) frozen green peas
2 cups	(340 g) diced cooked chicken

Shortcrust Pastry

In a bowl, whisk the egg white until frothy. Set aside.

In another bowl, combine the egg yolk, water and vinegar.

In a large bowl, combine the flour and salt. Add the vegetable shortening. Cut the shortening into the flour using a dough blender or two knives until it forms pea-sized pieces. Make a well at the center of the mixture. Pour the egg yolk mixture into the center of the well. Using a fork, gradually mix the dry and wet ingredients together until just moistened. Add the egg white and gently mix to combine.

Cut the dough into four equal parts. Shape each piece of dough into a disc with your hands. Cover with plastic wrap and refrigerate for 1 hour or freeze. Thaw out completely in the refrigerator before using. You will only need two discs for this recipe.

Béchamel

Meanwhile, in a pot over medium heat, melt the butter. Add the flour and cook for 1 minute while whisking. Add the green onions and cook for 10 seconds. Whisk in the broth and milk. Bring to a boil while whisking. Simmer gently for 2 minutes or until the sauce thickens. Season with salt and pepper. Remove from the heat and let cool.

Filling

In a small pot of boiling salted water, cook the carrots until tender. Add the peas and cook 1 minute longer. Drain well.

Add the vegetables and chicken to the pot of cooled béchamel. Mix well.

Assembly

With the rack in the lowest position, preheat the oven to 400°F (200°C).

On a lightly floured work surface, roll out two discs of dough until about ⅛ inch (3 mm) thick. Line a 9-inch (23 cm) round, 2-inch (5 cm) deep glass pie dish with one disc of dough. Make a few incisions in the center of the second disc.

Spread the chicken filling out in the bottom of the dough-lined pie dish. Brush the edge of the dough with milk.

Cover with the second disc of dough and remove any excess dough as needed. Fold the edge of the top disc under the bottom disc and seal together with your fingers or a fork. Freeze at this point, if desired (see note). Brush the surface of the pie with milk.

Bake for 1 hour or until the crust is nicely browned. Let sit for 45 minutes before serving to let the sauce thicken. Serve with Homemade Chunky Ketchup (p. 21), if desired.

| NOTE | You can bake the chicken pot pie from frozen in an oven preheated to 350°F (180°C) for 1 hour 30 minutes.

SUPER FLAKY CRUST The key to a good shortcrust pastry is simple enough: vegetable shortening. The addition of vinegar helps halt gluten production, gives a nice tangy finish and promotes flakiness. The result is a dough that's easy to handle and rolls out easily. It's practically foolproof and you'll have enough dough left over for a second pie.

SECRET'S IN THE SAUCE Yes, the chicken is important (and we prefer to use a roasted chicken, shredded by hand, rather than sautéed chicken) but a successful chicken pot pie is really all about the sauce. We want the sauce to be just runny enough, creamy and flavorful. The first step: chicken broth, for its taste, followed by milk, the key to its creaminess. And to thicken it just so, we use flour instead of cornstarch.

CLASSIC FILLING We're not reinventing the wheel with carrots and peas; they're classics. When it comes to peas, we prefer the frozen varieties as they hold their shape better than their canned counterparts. And we add a good amount of chicken so that you could really taste it. After all, it's the star of this dish.

Coquilles St. Jacques

PREPARATION 25 minutes
COOKING 35 minutes
SERVINGS 4
FREEZES WELL

Mashed Potatoes

2 cups	(340 g) peeled and cubed russet potatoes
2 tbsp	butter
2 tbsp	(30 ml) 35% cream

Scallop Filling

2	shallots, finely chopped
2 tbsp	butter
2 tbsp	unbleached all-purpose flour
½ cup	(125 ml) milk
¼ cup	(60 ml) dry white wine
11 oz	(300 g) medium scallops (15–25), thawed, drained and patted dry
1 cup	(100 g) grated Gruyère cheese

Mashed Potatoes

Place the potatoes in a pot. Cover with cold water. Season with salt. Bring to a boil. Simmer for 20 minutes or until the potatoes are very tender. Drain. Return to the pot. Using a potato masher, coarsely purée the potatoes with the butter.

Purée the mashed potatoes and 35% cream with an electric mixer until smooth. Add more cream as needed. Season with salt and pepper. Transfer to a pastry bag fitted with a large star tip.

With the rack in the middle position, preheat the oven to 350°F (180°C).

Scallop Filling

In another pot, soften the shallots in the butter. Season with salt and pepper. Add the flour and cook for 1 minute while whisking. Add the milk and wine. Bring to a boil while whisking. Cook for 1 minute. Remove from the heat.

Add the scallops and half of the Gruyère (½ cup/50 g) to the pot. Mix well.

Spoon the scallop filling into four scallop shells or small gratin dishes. Pipe rosettes of mashed potatoes around the edge of the filling. Sprinkle with the remaining Gruyère. Freeze at this point, if desired (see note). Place the shells or gratin dishes on a baking sheet. Transfer to the oven and bake for 10 minutes. Finish cooking under the broiler until the cheese and potatoes are golden.

| NOTE | **You can bake the Coquilles St. Jacques from frozen in an oven preheated to 350°F (180°C) by adding 4 to 5 minutes to the cooking time, or until the filling is heated through and the cheese and potatoes are golden, for a total of 14 to 15 minutes.**

ABOUT APPELLATION Coquilles St. Jacques isn't a recipe in France. It's rather the name of a mollusk (larger than a scallop), along with its shell. Here, Coquilles St. Jacques includes a white wine-based béchamel sauce, scallops and grated Gruyère, and is topped with mashed potatoes. Versions that feature shrimp or crab are named Coquille fruits de mer ("seafood").

PERFECT SCALLOPS You want to avoid overcooking your scallops, as this will make them rubbery. We therefore use scallops that are rather big in order to have better control over cooking. To do so, combine the scallops with the warm sauce right before placing them in the shell. Note that the way the scallops are cooked affects the creaminess of the sauce, because the seafood contains a certain amount of water, which is released during cooking.

CHOICE OF VESSEL We chose to cook this dish in the shell rather than a gratin dish. Given that the shell is porous, it absorbs the excess liquid released by the scallops as they cook. This has the same effect as a pizza cooked on a stone: the stone is porous and absorbs excess humidity for a crisp crust. The shell also acts as insulation, warming more slowly in the oven than a ceramic dish, which helps to better control the scallops' cooking.

Salmon Pot Pie

PREPARATION 1 hour
CHILLING 30 minutes
COOKING 1 hour 30 minutes
WAITING 15 minutes
SERVINGS 4 to 5
FREEZES WELL

Shortcrust Pastry

1½ cups	(225 g) unbleached all-purpose flour
½ tsp	baking powder
½ tsp	salt
½ cup	(115 g) cold unsalted butter, diced
3 tbsp	(45 ml) cold milk
1	egg

Filling

2 cups	(320 g) peeled and diced russet potatoes
4	garlic cloves, halved
¼ cup	(55 g) butter
1 cup	(95 g) chopped leek
¼ cup	(60 ml) 35% cream
1 lb	(450 g) salmon fillet without skin, cubed

Béchamel

2 tbsp	butter
2 tbsp	unbleached all-purpose flour
¾ cup	(180 ml) milk, plus more for brushing
½ cup	(50 g) grated sharp cheddar cheese

Shortcrust Pastry

In a food processor, blend the flour, baking powder and salt. Add the butter and pulse a few times, until it forms pea-sized pieces. Add the milk and egg. Pulse just until the dough starts coming together. Add more milk, as needed. Remove the dough from the food processor and shape into two discs with your hands. Cover with plastic wrap and refrigerate for 30 minutes.

Filling

Meanwhile, place the potatoes and garlic in a pot. Cover with cold water. Season with salt. Bring to a boil. Simmer for 15 minutes or until the potatoes are tender. Drain. Return to the pot. Using a potato masher, purée the potatoes and garlic with half of the butter (2 tbsp). Season with salt and pepper.

Meanwhile, in a large non-stick skillet over medium-high heat, soften the leek in the remaining butter. Add the 35% cream and salmon. Continue to cook, stirring often, until the salmon is cooked through and the cream has almost completely reduced. Transfer to the pot of mashed potatoes. Mix well to crumble the salmon. Adjust the seasoning. Set aside.

Béchamel

Meanwhile, in a small pot over medium heat, melt the butter. Add the flour and cook for 1 minute while whisking. Whisk in the milk. Bring to a boil while whisking. Simmer gently for 2 minutes or until the sauce thickens. Remove from the heat. Add the cheddar and stir until melted. Season with salt and pepper. Cover and set aside.

Assembly

With the rack in the lowest position, preheat the oven to 400°F (200°C).

On a lightly floured work surface, roll out the two discs of dough until about ⅛ inch (3 mm) thick. Line a 9-inch (23 cm) glass pie dish with one disc of dough. Make a few incisions in the center of the second disc.

Spread the salmon filling out in the bottom of the dough-lined pie dish. Cover with the béchamel.

Using a pastry brush, cover the edge of the dough with milk. Cover with the second disc of dough and remove any excess dough as needed. Fold the edge of the top disc under the bottom disc and seal together with your fingers or a fork. Freeze at this point, if desired (see note). Brush the surface of the pie with milk.

Bake for 45 minutes or until the crust is nicely browned. Let sit for 15 minutes before serving.

| NOTE | You can bake the salmon pot pie from frozen in an oven preheated to 350°F (180°C) for 1 hour 15 minutes.

FRESH FISH When making a proper salmon pie, there's no compromise: you must use fresh fish. It has a more delicate and subtle taste than its canned counterpart.

A GOOD CRUST Shortcrust pastry has a buttery taste and a crisp texture, and adding baking powder helps improve its flakiness. As for the egg, it makes the dough easy to roll out and creates a better hold when baking.

MASHED POTATOES Wanting to bring a soft texture to the pie, we mash the potatoes rather than dice them. We then mix them with the salmon in order to flake it well.

CREAMY BÉCHAMEL We replaced the traditional egg-based sauce that's normally served on top of the pie with a thin layer of béchamel sauce underneath the top pie crust. It adds moisture to the dish, preventing the dry sensation in the mouth common in some recipes. We also add a touch of aged cheddar to give the pie personality.

Veal Blanquette

PREPARATION 40 minutes
COOKING 2 hours 15 minutes
SERVINGS 6

3 lb	(1.4 kg) veal cubes (inside round)
1	onion, peeled
2	cloves
2	parsley sprigs
1	thyme sprig
1	bay leaf
2	carrots, cut into pieces
2	celery stalks, cut into pieces
2	garlic cloves, peeled
10 cups	(2.5 L) low-sodium chicken broth
1 bag	(284 g) small pearl onions, blanched 2 minutes and peeled
½ lb	(225 g) white mushrooms, sliced
6 tbsp	(85 g) butter
⅓ cup	(50 g) unbleached all-purpose flour
½ cup	(125 ml) 35% cream
1	egg yolk

Place the meat in a large pot. Cover with cold water. Bring to a boil and cook for 3 minutes. Drain. Rinse the meat under cold running water. Drain well. Wash out the pot. Return the meat to the clean pot.

Pierce the onion with the cloves. Using butcher's twine, tie the parsley, thyme and bay leaf together. Add the clove-studded onion to the pot of meat along with the bouquet garni (the bundle of herbs), carrots, celery, garlic and broth. Bring to a boil. Simmer gently, uncovered, for 1 hour 10 minutes or until the meat is tender but doesn't fall apart.

Meanwhile, in a non-stick skillet over medium-high heat, cook the pearl onions and mushrooms in 2 tbsp of the butter until starting to brown. Set aside.

Strain the broth through a sieve set over a bowl or large measuring cup. You will need 4 cups (1 L) of liquid. Add water to the broth as needed. Compost the vegetables and aromatics. Wash out the pot.

In the clean pot over medium heat, melt the remaining butter. Add the flour and cook for 1 minute while whisking. Gradually whisk in the broth. Bring to a boil while whisking. Simmer until the sauce thickens. Add the meat, pearl onions and mushrooms. Simmer over low heat for 5 minutes or until the onions are tender. Remove from the heat.

In a small bowl, combine the 35% cream and egg yolk. Just before serving, gradually stir the egg mixture into the blanquette. Add water to thin out the sauce as needed. Serve with Mashed Potatoes (p. 43) and green beans, if desired.

IMMACULATE SAUCE We wanted the sauce to be as white as possible for this recipe, as in the traditional French version. Many steps contribute to this, notably blanching the meat in water to get rid of the scum that appears during cooking. Cooking the onions and mushrooms separately prevents them from coloring the sauce. Finally, make sure to wash your pot between steps.

FLAVORFUL BROTH To make the homemade broth that acts as the base of the sauce, place an onion studded with cloves, a bouquet garni (parsley, thyme and a bay leaf tied together with string), and carrots, celery and garlic in the pot. All these aromatics serve to flavor the broth and are removed at the end.

WHITE ROUX Used to thicken sauces, the roux is a combination of equal parts butter and flour that are cooked. We like our roux to be as pale white as possible, so we cook it for no longer than a minute (which is enough time to remove the starchy taste) before adding the broth.

KEEP WARM Once the sauce is prepared, keep it warm before pouring in the cream and egg yolk, two ingredients that add creaminess. The residual heat will thicken the mixture. Avoid boiling the sauce, as you may cook the egg. We recommend adding the mixture to the hot sauce, off the heat, at the very last minute.

Steak *au Poivre*

PREPARATION 20 minutes
COOKING 20 minutes
WAITING 45 minutes
SERVINGS 4

2	beef striploin steaks, each about 11 oz (300 g) and 1½ inches (4 cm) thick
2 tbsp	black peppercorns, crushed
1 tbsp	(15 ml) vegetable oil
3 tbsp	butter
2	garlic cloves, halved
2	thyme sprigs
1	shallot, finely chopped
¼ cup	(60 ml) cognac or brandy
1 cup	(250 ml) 15% cooking cream or 35% cream

Place the steaks on a plate. Season generously with salt on all sides. Let sit at room temperature for 30 minutes.

Set aside 1 tsp of the crushed peppercorns for the sauce. Sprinkle the remaining pepper over both sides of the steaks, pressing down lightly.

Heat a cast-iron pan or another type of skillet (avoid non-stick) over medium-high heat until very hot. Cook the steaks in the oil for 3 minutes on each side for rare or until the desired doneness. Add the butter, garlic and thyme to the skillet. Once the butter is foaming, generously baste the steaks with the butter for 1 minute. Place the steaks on a clean plate. Let rest for 15 minutes. Remove the garlic and thyme from the skillet and compost them.

Meanwhile, in the same skillet over medium heat, soften the shallot and reserved peppercorns in the hot butter. Deglaze with the cognac. Let reduce until almost dry. Add the cream. Season lightly with salt. Simmer until the sauce is thick enough to coat the back of a spoon, 3 to 4 minutes. Adjust the seasoning.

Return the steaks and any cooking juices accumulated in the plate to the sauce. Baste the steaks with the sauce to reheat them.

On a work surface, slice the meat against the grain. Divide the steaks and sauce among four plates. Serve with Homemade Fries (p. 15), if desired.

EVEN COOKING One of the key first steps to a well-cooked steak is to salt it before cooking and let it sit for 30 minutes. The salt binds the water in the meat and makes it juicier once cooked. By tempering it, this helps achieve an even cooking throughout the steak (that is, no cold center!).

LOTS OF PEPPER A pepper steak should, obviously, contain an impressive amount of pepper! Even though there's plenty of it, the taste still remains well balanced. Add some of the peppercorns to the sauce and press the rest onto the surface of the meat just before cooking. It's best to use freshly crushed peppercorns instead of ground peppercorns to get the most aroma.

BUTTERY SAUCE Butter, thyme and garlic, added halfway through cooking, subtly perfume the meat. Let them infuse slowly; their flavor will act as the base of the sauce.

CONCENTRATED FLAVORS We use cognac to deglaze the pan. You can also use brandy, Armagnac or any other grape pomace-based alcohol. Reduce until it's almost dry before adding the cream; this is to emphasize the fruit notes of the cognac rather than the strong taste of the alcohol.

ALL ABOUT CREAM A pepper sauce just wouldn't be the same without cream, which rounds out the peppery flavor. We use a 15% cooking cream, as it's rich and silky without being too heavy.

Beef Tartare

PREPARATION 30 minutes
SERVINGS 4

1½ lb	(675 g) very fresh beef inside round roast (not tenderized)
2 tbsp	(30 ml) lemon juice
2 tbsp	(30 ml) Dijon mustard
1 tbsp	(15 ml) whole-grain mustard
1	egg yolk
1 tbsp	capers, chopped
2 tsp	(10 ml) sambal oelek, or more to taste
¼ cup	(60 ml) olive oil
3 tbsp	finely chopped shallots
3 tbsp	finely chopped chives
2 tbsp	finely chopped flat-leaf parsley

Fill a bowl two-thirds of the way up with ice. Place a second bowl over the ice. This will keep the meat very cold while you prepare the tartare.

On a work surface, using a knife, cut the meat into small dice and place in the chilled bowl as you go. Refrigerate.

In a third bowl, whisk together the lemon juice, Dijon mustard, whole-grain mustard, egg yolk, capers and sambal. Gradually whisk in the oil. Season with salt and pepper.

Add the mustard sauce, shallots, chives and parsley to the bowl of meat. Mix well. Adjust the seasoning.

Serve immediately with toasted baguette slices, Homemade Fries (p. 15) and green salad, if desired.

TENDER MEAT What you should look for in a tartare is meat that's tender and lean. Top round is a nice and surprising selection for us, as the meat is slightly more firm and considerably less expensive than filet mignon. Once cut into small dice, we can safely confirm that it's a great choice.

UNMATCHED FRESHNESS If you're thinking of making beef tartare using pre-ground meat, banish the thought from your mind! The freshness and quality of the meat used in this raw dish need to be impeccable. We recommend having your meat freshly cut by your butcher; be sure to inform them the intended use of the meat to ensure its freshness.

CHOP WITH A KNIFE For an enjoyable mouthfeel, be sure to finely chop the meat with a knife. Work with a well-sharpened knife for a clean cut every time. Avoid using a meat grinder, which will turn your meat into mush, and avoid the stand mixer at all costs.

SEASON WELL When it comes to seasonings, we opt for classic flavors like herbs, capers, shallots, mustard and a touch of chili pepper. As for the sauce, we don't include mayonnaise as it tends to whiten the meat. Instead we use a sauce lightly emulsified with an egg yolk, along with olive oil and lemon juice for acidity.

Salmon Tartare

PREPARATION 30 minutes
SERVINGS 4

1½ lb	(675 g) very fresh salmon fillet without skin
4 tsp	finely chopped shallots
2 tbsp	(30 ml) white wine vinegar
1 tbsp	(15 ml) water
3 tbsp	(45 ml) olive oil
2 tbsp	finely chopped chives
4 tsp	(20 ml) lemon juice
1 tbsp	finely chopped flat-leaf parsley
1 tbsp	(15 ml) whole-grain mustard
1 tbsp	capers, chopped
1 tsp	(5 ml) hot sauce, or more to taste

Fill a bowl two-thirds of the way up with ice. Place a second bowl over the ice. This will keep the fish very cold while you prepare the tartare.

On a work surface, using a knife, cut the salmon into small dice and place in the chilled bowl as you go. Refrigerate.

In a small bowl, combine the shallots, vinegar and water. Let sit for 5 minutes. Drain the shallots and discard the liquid.

Add the shallots, oil, chives, lemon juice, parsley, mustard, capers and hot sauce to the bowl of salmon. Season with salt and pepper. Mix well.

Serve immediately with green salad, toasted baguette slices or plain potato chips, if desired.

SUBTLE DRESSING Most tartares rely on mayonnaise. We tried it but felt it overpowered the delicate fish. So we pay homage here to the tender salmon with a light vinaigrette of oil and lemon juice. The result: beautiful fruity inflections with overall subtlety.

CLASSIC SEASONINGS For this recipe, we decided to go back to the basics of French cuisine. So to highlight the fresh taste of the salmon, we use timeless flavors like parsley, shallots and mustard.

CHOICE CONDIMENTS We crave green, bright flavors like chives and parsley with our fresh fish. A handful of plump capers lends a salty punch, and whole-grain mustard brings some sweetness. We finish with a splash of hot sauce for a touch of heat.

MILD SHALLOTS Despite their pronounced flavors, we pair chives with shallots. To soften the taste of the latter, we chop and soak them in a bath of water and white wine vinegar for 5 minutes before folding them into the mix. The result: less kick, and a more mellow, complex flavor.

MIX OF FLAVORS AND TEXTURES From whole mustard seeds that pop in your mouth to succulent diced salmon, the irresistible variety of textures will take you on a flavor adventure.

Ratatouille

PREPARATION 30 minutes
COOKING 1 hour
COOLING 15 minutes
MAKES 6 cups (1.5 L)
FREEZES WELL

1	garlic bulb
5 cups	(700 g) cherry tomatoes or 1 can (28 oz/796 ml) diced tomatoes, drained
5	thyme sprigs
½ cup	(125 ml) olive oil
2	medium eggplants, peeled and diced
1	onion, chopped
2	zucchini, diced
2	red, yellow or orange bell peppers, seeded and diced
	Basil leaves, to taste

With the rack in the middle position, preheat the oven to 350°F (180°C).

On a work surface, cut off the top of the garlic bulb to expose the cloves.

In a Dutch oven or large ovenproof pot, place the garlic bulb, tomatoes and thyme. Drizzle with 2 tbsp (30 ml) of the oil. Season with salt and pepper. Cover and bake for 30 minutes or until the garlic is tender.

Meanwhile, in a large skillet over medium-high heat, brown half of the eggplant at a time in 2 tbsp (30 ml) of the oil. Season with salt and pepper. Set aside in a bowl.

In the same skillet, brown the onion, zucchini and bell peppers in the remaining oil. Season with salt and pepper.

Remove the pot from the oven and remove the lid. Add the sautéed vegetables and mix well. Cover and continue to bake for 30 minutes.

Remove the pot from the oven and remove the lid. Place the garlic bulb on a plate. Let cool for 15 minutes. Remove and compost the thyme sprigs.

Squeeze the garlic bulb with your hands to extract the roasted cloves and mix into the vegetables. Compost the garlic skin. Adjust the seasoning. Transfer the ratatouille to a serving dish. Garnish with basil leaves.

Serve the ratatouille alongside fish, meat or pasta or on its own with toasted bread and cheese.

CONFIT GARLIC Use a whole garlic bulb in this recipe, bake it in the oven until soft, then squeeze it to remove the roasted cloves. This roasted garlic imparts a well-rounded flavor and a slightly sweet taste, which enhances the ratatouille.

SUCCULENT VEGGIES Alongside the garlic, the tomatoes are roasted with thyme sprigs, to concentrate their flavor and highlight their sweet side. This also keeps them from releasing too much water afterwards in the ratatouille. As for the eggplant, make sure to peel it to avoid any bitterness. Then dice all the vegetables so that they cook evenly and the ratatouille is perfectly stewed.

COOK TWICE For optimal color, brown half of the eggplant at a time, keeping it separate from the other vegetables. Once perfectly browned, bake it in the oven to concentrate the flavor, resulting in very fragrant, almost confit-style vegetables.

RICH OLIVE OIL Olive oil is an essential ingredient in a ratatouille. Use a good amount to cook the vegetables, particularly the eggplant, which soaks it up like a sponge. Select a quality product to bring improved taste and richness to your ratatouille.

Clam Chowder

PREPARATION 30 minutes
COOKING 45 minutes
WAITING 15 minutes
SERVINGS 4

1	onion, finely chopped
1	small leek, white part only, chopped
3 tbsp	butter
3 tbsp	unbleached all-purpose flour
2 bottles	(236 ml each) clam juice
3 cups	(750 ml) milk
2 cups	(320 g) peeled and diced potatoes
3	bay leaves
1 pinch	ground nutmeg
1½ cups	(225 g) corn kernels, blanched (from about 2 ears corn)
2 cans	(142 g each) small whole clams, drained (discard the juice)
5 oz	(140 g) bacon, diced
20	small fresh clams, cleaned (optional)
¼ cup	(60 ml) water
2 tbsp	finely chopped chives

In a large pot over medium heat, soften the onion and leek in the butter until translucent, about 10 minutes. Add the flour and continue to cook for 1 minute while stirring. Add the clam juice. Bring to a boil, stirring constantly.

Add the milk, potatoes, bay leaves and nutmeg to the pot. Bring to a boil, stirring constantly. Simmer over medium heat for 20 minutes or until the potatoes are tender. Add the corn and continue to cook for 2 minutes. Remove from the heat.

Add the canned clams to the pot. Season with salt and pepper. Mix well. Let sit for at least 15 minutes before serving. Remove and compost the bay leaves.

Meanwhile, in a small skillet over medium heat, cook the bacon until nicely browned but still tender. Drain the bacon on a plate lined with paper towels. Keep 1 tbsp (15 ml) of the bacon fat in the skillet. Add three-quarters of the bacon to the soup.

In the same skillet, toss the fresh clams with the hot bacon fat. Add the water. Cover and bring to a boil. Cook for 3 to 5 minutes or until the clams have opened. Remove the clams from the liquid (discard any clams that have not opened).

Divide the soup among four bowls. Garnish with the fresh clams and remaining bacon and sprinkle with the chives. This chowder is delicious served with crackers.

DELICATE FLAVOR In many variations of chowder, a good amount of vegetables are included; we set aside the more commonly used carrots and celery for this recipe in favor of corn with its slightly sweet taste. We also add a bit of nutmeg and bay leaf, just enough to fragrance the broth. We're aiming for plenty of flavor while still letting the delicate taste of the clams shine.

CHOOSE BACON WISELY For this recipe, we prefer bacon cut into pieces rather than slices. And we want a softer texture, which is why we brown the bacon without letting it get crispy. Avoid maple wood smoked bacon, as its strong flavor could overpower the dish.

CANNED CLAMS It can be difficult to find fresh clams that aren't full of sand, which is why we use pre-washed canned clams instead. We also enjoy the softness and affordability of the yellow clam variety. If you want to include fresh clams, add them as a garnish.

REST TIME Given that the chowder is thickened with flour, it tends to get thicker over time. We recommend letting it rest for 15 minutes before serving, and then adding a bit of water or broth if needed to thin. The soup will thicken even more after it's been in the refrigerator. Gently reheat until it reaches a liquid consistency.

Hunter's Chicken Stew

PREPARATION 20 minutes
WAITING 15 minutes
COOKING 1 hour 30 minutes
SERVINGS 4
FREEZES WELL

½ oz	(14 g) dried bolete (or porcini) mushrooms
1½ cups	(375 ml) beef broth
4	whole chicken legs (see note)
1 tbsp	(15 ml) olive oil
½ lb	(225 g) white mushrooms, quartered
½ lb	(225 g) oyster mushrooms, thinly sliced
2 tbsp	butter
1	onion, chopped
2	garlic cloves, chopped
2 tbsp	unbleached all-purpose flour
½ cup	(125 ml) dry white wine
1	small tomato, seeded and diced
1 tsp	finely chopped tarragon leaves

In a small bowl of water, quickly rinse the dried mushrooms to remove any sand. Using a slotted spoon, remove the mushrooms from the water. Discard the water.

In a small pot, bring the broth to a boil. Remove from the heat. Add the dried mushrooms and let sit for 15 minutes to rehydrate. Using the slotted spoon, remove the mushrooms from the pot. Set the mushrooms and broth aside separately.

Meanwhile, on a work surface, remove and compost the chicken skin. With a knife, separate the thighs from the drumsticks.

In a Dutch oven or large pot over medium-high heat, brown the chicken in the oil on both sides. Season with salt and pepper. Set aside in a bowl.

Deglaze the pot with ¼ cup (60 ml) of the reserved broth, scraping the bottom of the pot with a wooden spoon. Pour over the chicken.

In the same pot over medium-high heat, brown the white mushrooms and oyster mushrooms in the butter. Add the rehydrated mushrooms, onion and garlic. Continue to cook for 2 minutes while stirring. Sprinkle with the flour and toss to coat well. Deglaze with the wine and let reduce by half, stirring gently with a whisk. Add the remaining broth, the tomato and chicken. Bring to a boil. Cover and simmer for 1 hour over low heat or until the chicken easily falls away from the bone.

Remove the lid. Let the sauce reduce for 5 minutes or until thick enough to coat the back of a spoon. Adjust the seasoning. Sprinkle with the tarragon. Serve with buttered noodles, if desired.

| NOTE | The whole chicken legs can be replaced with 4 bone-in drumsticks and 4 bone-in thighs.

BEEF EFFECT This Renaissance-era dish, originally made with game meat, was a rich stew popular with hunters. To give this recipe a richness reminiscent of yesteryear, we chose beef broth to add body and complexity.

MUSHROOM TRIO Hunters had a habit, while hunting game, of also foraging for mushrooms on the forest floor. At the end of the day, both found their way into the pot. Our recipe features three varieties of mushrooms: dried boletes or porcini, white and oyster. Together, they bring texture and umami (the fifth taste), and the rehydration liquid of the boletes or porcini provides character to the stew.

DARK MEAT We use dark meat (specifically that of chicken thighs) in this recipe for a couple of reasons. First, bone-in thighs impart that rich and generous flavor that is sought after in stews. Second, the texture of dark meat is conducive to a slow cooking time. We prefer to remove the skin before cooking, as it adds too much fat to the sauce and becomes rubbery as it is cooked.

BALANCE OF FLAVORS Traditional chicken stews generally call for a dry white wine or a vermouth—a fruity white would simply ruin all the layers of umami flavor, whereas a dry white with clear acidity brings more balance. The same intention of balance goes for the moderate use of tomatoes (you only need one) and the fresh touch of tarragon reminiscent of aniseed.

Coq au Vin

PREPARATION 30 minutes
MARINATING 12 hours
COOKING 1 hour 30 minutes
SERVINGS 4
FREEZES WELL

1	whole chicken, about 4 lb (1.8 kg), cut into 8 pieces
2 cups	(500 ml) red wine
1	thyme sprig
1	rosemary sprig
6 tbsp	(85 g) butter, softened
¼ lb	(115 g) thick bacon slices, diced
1	onion, chopped
2	garlic cloves, chopped
1 tbsp	(15 ml) tomato paste
2 tbsp	(30 ml) cognac or brandy
1½ cups	(375 ml) chicken broth
1	bay leaf
2 tbsp	unbleached all-purpose flour
½ lb	(225 g) white mushrooms, quartered
6 oz	(170 g) small pearl onions, blanched 2 minutes and peeled
2 tbsp	finely chopped flat-leaf parsley

In a glass dish, combine the chicken pieces, wine, thyme and rosemary. Cover and let marinate in the refrigerator for 12 hours or overnight, turning the chicken over once or twice, if possible.

Drain the chicken through a strainer set over a bowl. Set the marinade aside. Compost the herbs. Pat the chicken dry with paper towels.

In a large non-stick skillet over medium-high heat, brown the chicken in 2 tbsp of the butter. Season with salt and pepper. Set aside on a large plate.

In a Dutch oven or large pot over medium heat, brown the bacon in 1 tbsp of the butter. Add the onion and garlic. Cook for 2 minutes. Add the tomato paste and cook for 1 minute while stirring. Deglaze with the cognac. Add the broth and reserved marinade. Let the sauce reduce by one-third. Add the chicken and bay leaf. Cover and simmer over medium-low heat for 1 hour or until the chicken easily detaches from the bone.

Meanwhile, in a small bowl, combine 2 tbsp of the butter with the flour. Set aside.

In the same skillet used to sear the chicken over medium-high heat, brown the mushrooms and pearl onions in the remaining butter. Season with salt and pepper.

Using a slotted spoon, remove the chicken and bacon from the sauce. Set aside on a large clean plate. Bring the sauce to a boil over medium heat. Whisk in the butter-flour mixture until the sauce thickens. Return the chicken and bacon to the pot. Add the mushrooms and pearl onions. Simmer for 5 minutes. Adjust the seasoning. Sprinkle with the parsley. Serve with egg noodles, if desired.

POWERFUL WINE Light red wines are traditionally used for marinating the poultry; some versions suggest white wine, or even champagne. Our tests with a more robust red wine yielded good results, and we eventually decided on a full-bodied grape variety being best, like a Syrah. Along with its flavor, it gives both the meat and sauce a lovely tint.

A HINT OF SMOKE What's best, salt pork or bacon? We found that both work well so it's really a matter of preference. We call for bacon here as it infuses the sauce, giving it greater depth and nuance.

LONG MARINATION We took our cue from civet (a traditional French stew of rabbit or game), where ample marinating time helps to tenderize the meat, and found that soaking the chicken in the red wine and herbs for 12 hours yields perfect results. The aroma and color of the wine seep right to the bone.

DOUBLE REDUCTION The liquids in this recipe are reduced not once, but twice. The first reduction evaporates the alcohol and concentrates the flavors. The second lightly cooks the flour and thickens the sauce.

For 6 people: 4½ lb (2 kg) roast

Cooking time in a 500°F (260°C) oven = 25 minutes

For 10 to 12 people: 8 lb (3.6 kg) roast

Cooking time in a 500°F (260°C) oven = 40 minutes

For 14 to 16 people: 11 lb (5 kg) roast

Cooking time in a 500°F (260°C) oven = 55 minutes

Continue with the 2-hour slow-roasting process.

Prime Rib Roast with Béarnaise Sauce

PREPARATION 25 minutes
COOKING 2 hours 25 minutes
SERVINGS 6

Rib Roast

1 tbsp	unbleached all-purpose flour
1 tsp	salt
1 tsp	ground black pepper
1 tsp	onion powder
½ tsp	garlic powder
1	bone-in prime rib beef roast, about 4½ lb (2 kg), at room temperature for 1 hour

Béarnaise Sauce

½ cup	(125 ml) white wine
¼ cup	(60 ml) white wine vinegar
2	shallots, chopped
1	tarragon sprig
4	egg yolks
¾ cup	(170 g) unsalted butter, melted and cooled
1 tbsp	finely chopped tarragon leaves

Rib Roast

With the rack in the middle position, preheat the oven to 500°F (260°C). Line a baking sheet with foil.

In a bowl, combine the flour, salt, pepper, onion powder and garlic powder.

On a work surface, rub the roast all over with the seasoning mixture.

Place the roast on the prepared baking sheet, fat-side up. Bake for 25 minutes (see the page opposite for how to cook a roast over 4½ lb/2 kg).

Turn the oven off and do not open the door for 2 hours (it is very important not to release any heat from the oven during this time). Remove the roast from the oven. On a work surface, slice the roast.

Béarnaise Sauce

Meanwhile, in a small pot, bring the wine, vinegar, shallots and tarragon sprig to a boil. Season with pepper. Let reduce until only about 3 tbsp (45 ml) of liquid remains. Strain through a sieve set over a bowl. Compost the residue.

Add the egg yolks to the bowl of wine reduction and whisk to combine. Place the bowl over a pot of simmering water and whisk until the sauce is thick and foamy. Do not overcook the sauce to avoid coagulating the eggs.

Remove the bowl from the pot. Off the heat, slowly whisk in the melted butter. Add the chopped tarragon. Adjust the seasoning. If the sauce is too thick, whisk in a little hot water. Set aside at room temperature. When ready to serve, place back over the pot of simmering water and whisk for a few seconds to reheat.

Serve the meat and Béarnaise sauce with Mashed Potatoes (p. 43) and vegetables, if desired.

THE RIGHT ROAST You want to use a bone-in roast for this recipe, but as a premium cut it is quite expensive, so watch for sales. Calling your butcher ahead to check availability is also a good idea. You'll need about 7 to 12 oz (200 to 350 g) per person, depending on appetites.

THE RUB Salt, pepper, a bit of flour, onion powder and garlic powder are the only ingredients required. Mix in a bowl, then rub it evenly all over the roast. The flour helps form a nice crust on the outside.

PRECIOUS COOKING First, to create that gorgeous crust and develop a deep color, the roast is cooked in the center of a 500°F (260°C) oven for 25 to 55 minutes (see sidebar). Then, the oven is turned off and the 2-hour-long slow-roasting process begins. Don't open the oven door; the residual heat is what cooks the meat while maintaining moisture.

MEDIUM RARE Once the time has elapsed, it's ready to serve. There's no need to cover the roast or let it rest. If you need to buy a little time, it can be left in the oven for an hour more at most.

Beef Bourguignon

PREPARATION 30 minutes
COOKING 2 hours
SERVINGS 6
FREEZES WELL

Beef

3 tbsp	butter, softened
3 tbsp	unbleached all-purpose flour
5 oz	(140 g) salt pork, rind removed and diced
2½ lb	(1.1 kg) chuck roast or boneless beef blade roast, cubed
2 tbsp	(30 ml) olive oil
1	large onion, chopped
1	carrot, diced
2	garlic cloves, chopped
3 tbsp	(45 ml) brandy
2 cups	(500 ml) red wine
2 cups	(500 ml) beef broth
1	thyme sprig
1	bay leaf

Toppings

½ lb	(225 g) white mushrooms, halved
6 oz	(170 g) small pearl onions, blanched 2 minutes and peeled
3 tbsp	butter
2 tbsp	finely chopped parsley leaves

Beef

With the rack in the middle position, preheat the oven to 325°F (165°C).

In a small bowl, combine the butter and flour. Set aside.

In a small pot of boiling water, blanch the salt pork for 5 minutes to remove some of the salt. Drain. Set aside on a plate lined with paper towels.

In a Dutch oven or large ovenproof pot over medium-high heat, brown half of the beef at a time in the oil. Season with salt and pepper. Set aside on another plate. Pour the cooking fat into a glass bowl.

In the same pot, brown the onion, carrot and salt pork in 1 tbsp (15 ml) of the beef cooking fat. Once cooled, compost the remaining cooking fat. Add the garlic to the pot and cook for 1 minute while stirring. Add the brandy and let reduce until almost dry. Add the wine and let reduce by half. Whisk in the broth and the butter-flour mixture. Bring to a boil. Return the beef to the pot. Add the thyme and bay leaf. Cover and transfer to the oven. Bake for 1 hour.

Toppings

Meanwhile, in a large skillet over high heat, cook the mushrooms and pearl onions in the butter until nicely browned. Season with salt and pepper.

Remove the pot from the oven and remove the lid. Add the mushrooms and onions. Mix well. Cover and continue to bake for 30 minutes or until the beef is tender. Adjust the seasoning. Remove and compost the thyme and bay leaf.

Divide the beef Bourguignon among six plates. Garnish with the parsley. Serve with pappardelle pasta, potatoes or, for a more traditional accompaniment, toasted and buttered crusty bread.

CUT OF MEAT We use a chuck roast that comes from the shoulder here, but if your butcher doesn't have any, a boneless beef blade roast will suffice. Our tests showed that these two cuts had different textures once cooked: cubed beef blade tended to shred, while the chuck cubes kept their shape.

SOAK THAT SALT PORK It's common to find salt pork in traditional versions, as it brings plenty of flavor to the dish. By soaking it in water to remove the salt, you'll get a more balanced flavor.

ADD ALCOHOL As is customary, we included wine in this recipe. Just a small amount adds a complexity and depth of flavor to the sauce in which the meat is cooked.

COOK IN CAST-IRON You can use any oven-safe pot, but a cast-iron one yields the best results, as it browns the beef cubes perfectly and distributes heat evenly. Plus, cooking the meat in the oven rather than on the stovetop ensures even more consistent results

---

Swiss Cheese Fondue

PREPARATION 15 minutes
COOKING 1 hour 45 minutes
SERVINGS 4

5 cups	(500 g) grated Gruyère cheese
1½ cups	(150 g) grated Emmental cheese
1½ cups	(150 g) grated Vacherin cheese
4 tsp	cornstarch
	Freshly grated nutmeg, to taste
2	small garlic cloves, slightly crushed
1½ cups	(375 ml) Riesling or other dry white wine
4 tsp	(20 ml) kirsch (optional)

In a large bowl, combine the Gruyère, Emmental and Vacherin cheese with the cornstarch. Season with pepper and nutmeg.

Rub the inside of a fondue pot with 1 garlic clove. On a work surface, finely chop the 2 garlic cloves and place in the pot. Add the wine and the cheese mixture.

Heat the fondue pot over medium heat, stirring constantly with a wooden spoon, until the cheese has melted and the mixture is smooth. Simmer very gently for 30 seconds. Stir in the kirsch. Adjust the seasoning.

Place a fondue heating plate at the center of the table. Select the Cheese function and set the fondue pot on the heating plate.

Serve the cheese fondue with your choice of cubed country bread, pieces of green apple, fresh grapes, cubed ham, cherry tomatoes, blanched broccoli florets and slices of cooked or dried sausage.

CHEESE SELECTION There are numerous variations to try here: half Emmental, half Gruyère is a traditional choice. Some enjoy adding Vacherin, Appenzell or even cheddar cheese. In our recipe, just like in the classic Swiss version, we made Gruyère the star but went with one that's been cave aged, giving it a more intense flavor than its regular counterpart. We also included Emmental and Vacherin.

TRADITIONAL FLAVORS Black pepper and nutmeg are classic aromatics. Garlic is normally used to rub the inside of the fondue pot, but we chose to add it to the mixture as well. It helps enhance the flavors of the cheese without being too overpowering, which is great for those who aren't too fond of garlic.

ALL AT ONCE We've always been told to add the cheese gradually and let it melt before adding more. Not in this recipe! We found we could add the ingredients all at once as long as we stirred continuously.

GET DIPPING! Cubed bread is a cheese fondue staple. Should you choose fresh or stale? Stale is standard, but feel free to go with your own preference. And if you find eating bread exclusively is a bit heavy, other lighter sides include fruits (green apple, grapes) and vegetables (blanched broccoli or cauliflower, cherry tomatoes).

Chocolate
Chocolat
Cheese
Fromage
Broth
Bouillon

Fried Chicken

PREPARATION 30 minutes
MARINATING 12 hours
COOKING 45 minutes
SERVINGS 6

Marinade

2 cups	(500 ml) buttermilk
1½ tsp	salt
1½ tsp	onion powder
1½ tsp	garlic powder
1 tsp	cayenne pepper
½ tsp	ground allspice
8	bone-in chicken drumsticks with skin
8	bone-in chicken thighs with skin

Coating

	Vegetable oil, for frying
3 cups	(450 g) unbleached all-purpose flour
1½ tsp	salt
1½ tsp	onion powder
1½ tsp	garlic powder
1½ tsp	dry mustard
1½ tsp	smoked paprika
1½ tsp	cayenne pepper

Spicy Mayonnaise

1 cup	(250 ml) mayonnaise
1 tbsp	(15 ml) sambal oelek
1 tsp	(5 ml) honey

Marinade

In a bowl, combine the buttermilk, salt, onion powder, garlic powder, cayenne and allspice. Add the chicken and toss to coat well with the marinade. Cover and refrigerate for 12 hours or overnight.

Coating

Preheat the oil in a deep fryer to 325°F (165°C). Line a baking sheet with paper towels or set a wire rack on it. Preheat the oven to 200°F (95°C).

In a large bowl, combine the flour, salt, onion powder, garlic powder, mustard, paprika and cayenne.

Remove the chicken from the marinade without letting it all drip off. Dredge the chicken in the flour mixture, shaking off any excess. Dip for a second time in the marinade and dredge again in the flour mixture, shaking off any excess. Set aside on another baking sheet.

Fry 4 or 5 pieces of chicken at a time in the hot oil for 15 minutes or until a thermometer inserted in the center of a piece without touching bone reads 180°F (82°C), turning the chicken over a few times during cooking. Watch out for splattering. Drain on the prepared baking sheet. Keep the chicken warm in the oven while you fry the remaining pieces.

Spicy Mayonnaise

Meanwhile, in a bowl, combine the mayonnaise, sambal and honey. Serve the spicy mayonnaise with the fried chicken.

THE TASTE OF BUTTER The key to fried chicken's flavor is the marinade, and we particularly love using buttermilk. Its enzymes and acidity help tenderize the meat while coating it in a flavor reminiscent of buttered popcorn.

WELL-BALANCED MARINADE If you want big flavor in your marinade, don't hesitate to add a good amount of spices. As for salt, it's essential: it's what helps the marinade penetrate deep into the meat for a tender, juicy texture when cooked.

IDEAL BREADING For crispy skin with just a bit of a kick, we opt for smoked paprika. It's a great addition, as its flavor is strong but agreeable. As for the coating, we use white flour for a crunchy breading.

COOK UNTIL GOLDEN While vegetable shortening for frying yields a very crisp skin, we chose vegetable oil here, which yields a perfectly golden and more appetizing chicken. We recommend a deep fryer temperature of 325°F (165°C), as anything higher will burn the crust and leave your chicken unevenly cooked.

General Tao Tofu

PREPARATION 25 minutes
COOKING 15 minutes
SERVINGS 4

Sauce

¼ cup	(55 g) brown sugar
¼ cup	(60 ml) vegetable or chicken broth
2 tbsp	(30 ml) low-sodium soy sauce
2 tbsp	(30 ml) rice vinegar
2 tbsp	(30 ml) ketchup
1 tsp	cornstarch
1 tsp	(5 ml) sambal oelek

Stir-Fry

1 lb	(450 g) firm tofu, patted very dry and cubed
2 tbsp	cornstarch
¼ cup	(60 ml) vegetable oil
4	green onions, finely chopped
2	garlic cloves, finely chopped
1 tsp	finely chopped fresh ginger
	Cilantro leaves, to taste

Sauce

In a bowl, whisk together all of the ingredients. Set aside.

Stir-Fry

In a large bowl, dredge the tofu in the cornstarch, shaking off any excess. Set aside on a plate.

In a wok over medium-high heat, warm the oil. Fry half of the tofu at a time until golden. Season with salt and pepper. Using a slotted spoon, remove the tofu from the wok and drain on a plate lined with paper towels.

In the same wok over medium heat, soften the green onions, garlic and ginger for 1 to 2 minutes while stirring. Add more oil as needed. Add the sauce and bring to a boil while stirring. Add the tofu and continue to cook for 2 minutes, stirring until warmed through and coated with the sauce.

Divide the tofu mixture among four plates. Garnish with cilantro leaves. Serve with jasmine rice and steamed broccoli, if desired.

FINDING BALANCE For the sauce to be sweet enough (but not too sweet!), it needs to strike the balance with its acidic side. We found this harmony by adding rice vinegar to the brown sugar. Then adding ketchup provides a mild taste and a coating aspect, all while adding a subtle hue to the sauce.

CHOP OR GRATE? We chose fresh ginger for this sauce for a touch of heat, but a subtle one. That's why we chop it finely rather than grate it—grating ginger intensifies its flavor, which was something we wanted to avoid here.

CORNSTARCH COATING The tofu's crispy texture is thanks to cornstarch. Coating the diced tofu in cornstarch creates a thin and delicate crust when seared, making the cubes perfectly golden and crisp on the outside. Be sure to pat the block of tofu dry before slicing into it, to keep the cornstarch from clumping in some spots.

LITTLE OIL Cook with a small amount of oil, just enough to sauté the tofu rather than fry it. The latter will make it too oily and greasy, which isn't what you want in this recipe.

QUICK AND EASY SAUCE You'll love how fuss-free this dish is, as you make the sauce right in the same pan you use to cook the tofu. The sauce thickens quickly and develops a coating texture thanks to the combined action of the cornstarch, both on the tofu and in the sauce.

Portuguese-Style Grilled Chicken

PREPARATION 30 minutes
COOKING 1 hour 45 minutes
MARINATING 12 hours
SERVINGS 4
FREEZES WELL

Spicy Sauce

2	shallots, thinly sliced
½ cup	(125 ml) olive oil
2 tbsp	(30 ml) piri piri sauce
2 tbsp	sweet paprika
½ cup	(125 ml) dry white wine
½ cup	(125 ml) chicken broth
½ cup	(115 g) unsalted butter, softened
2	garlic cloves, chopped

Chicken

1	whole chicken, about 4 lb (1.8 kg)
4 tsp	coarse sea salt
½	lemon

Spicy Sauce

In a small pot over high heat, brown the shallots in half of the oil (1⁄4 cup/60 ml). Add the piri piri sauce and paprika. Continue to cook for 1 minute while stirring. Add the remaining oil, the wine, broth and butter. Simmer for 15 minutes or until the sauce thickens slightly. Add the garlic and continue to cook for 1 minute. Transfer to a bowl and let cool.

Chicken

On a work surface, using a chef's knife or kitchen shears, cut out the backbone of the chicken. Open the chicken and spread it out flat.

Season both sides of the chicken with the salt. Rub with the cut-side of the lemon for 3 minutes or until the salt begins to dissolve. Let the chicken sit for 5 minutes.

Place the chicken in a large glass baking dish. Coat with 1⁄4 cup (60 ml) of the spicy sauce. Cover with plastic wrap and refrigerate for 12 hours or overnight. Cover the remaining sauce and refrigerate.

Preheat the grill, setting the burners to high. Oil the grate.

Turn off one side of the barbecue. Drain the chicken from the marinade and place flat and skin-side down on the side of the grill that is off. Close the lid. Grill for 45 minutes.

Flip the chicken over and continue to grill for 30 minutes or until a thermometer inserted in the thigh without touching bone reads 180°F (82°C). Finish by crisping up the skin on the heated side of the grill, if desired.

Meanwhile, in a small pot, reheat the remaining spicy sauce. On a work surface, cut the chicken into pieces. Brush generously with the sauce.

ON THE GRAVY TRAIN Cooking fat from the chicken is traditionally used to make the gravy, but for our spicy sauce, we combined butter with olive oil and chicken broth to make the job easier. The results were exactly what we were after: a velvety-smooth sauce with just the right balance of chicken flavor.

LIKE A BUTTERFLY Following the time-honored Portuguese method, we place our chicken flat on the grill. This butterflied (or spatchcocked) style allows fast and even cooking, and ensures that both the breast and legs are perfectly juicy. What's more, it makes it easier to douse the bird with the marinade.

TENDERIZE THE MEAT Salt plays an essential role in helping lock in moisture, which guarantees more tender meat. After giving it a good sprinkling of salt, we rub the whole chicken with half a lemon. This allows the salt to properly dissolve into the poultry.

SPICE IS NICE We wanted to finish the chicken with a marinade that brings the heat without overpowering everything else. This spicy Portuguese classic made with piri piri peppers was a no-brainer, but we toned it down a little by adding shallots, white wine and sweet paprika. It's important to marinate the chicken for at least 12 hours.

Chicken Shish Taouk

PREPARATION 30 minutes
MARINATING 8 hours
COOKING 35 minutes
SERVINGS 4

Garlic Sauce

3	large garlic cloves, quartered
2	egg whites
2 tbsp	(30 ml) lemon juice
½ tsp	salt
1½ cups	(375 ml) vegetable oil
3 tbsp	(45 ml) water

Chicken

3 tbsp	(45 ml) 35% cream
2 tbsp	(30 ml) vegetable oil
1 tbsp	(15 ml) lemon juice
¼ tsp	Lebanese seven-spice powder or ground allspice
¼ tsp	dried thyme
½ tsp	salt
1½ lb	(675 g) boneless, skinless chicken breasts (about 3 breasts)

Vermicelli Rice

½ cup	(80 g) short wheat vermicelli
2 tbsp	(30 ml) olive oil
1 cup	(200 g) basmati rice, rinsed and drained
1⅔ cups	(400 ml) water

Garlic Sauce

In a tall, narrow container (such as a measuring cup), place the garlic, egg whites, lemon juice and salt. Using a hand blender, purée the ingredients until smooth. With the machine running, slowly drizzle in 1 cup (250 ml) of the oil. The emulsion will begin to form a mayonnaise in less than 1 minute. With the machine still running, add the water alternating with the remaining oil. The garlic sauce will keep for 1 week in an airtight container in the refrigerator.

Chicken

In a bowl, whisk together ⅓ cup (75 ml) of the garlic sauce with the 35% cream, oil, lemon juice, seven-spice powder, thyme and salt. Season with pepper. Add the chicken and toss to coat with the marinade. Cover and refrigerate for 8 to 12 hours or overnight.

Vermicelli Rice

In a pot over medium-high heat, brown the vermicelli in the oil for 2 to 3 minutes, stirring constantly. Add the rice and cook for 30 seconds, stirring to coat with the oil. Add the water. Season with salt. Bring to a boil. Cover and simmer over low heat for 15 minutes or until the liquid is completely absorbed. Remove from the heat and let sit, covered, for 5 minutes.

Remove the lid of the pot and fluff the grains of rice with a fork. Adjust the seasoning.

Meanwhile, preheat the grill, setting the burners to medium-high. Oil the grate.

Grill the chicken for 7 to 8 minutes on each side or until a thermometer inserted in the center of a breast reads 165°F (74°C). The chicken should be nicely marked and caramelized on the surface. Let sit for 5 minutes on a plate. On a work surface, slice the chicken.

Serve the chicken on plates with the garlic sauce and vermicelli rice. Delicious served with green salad. The chicken is also great in pita sandwiches.

PERFECTLY MEASURED GARLIC The garlic sauce (called toum) completes the shish taouk and is a marinade component, so it needs to be perfectly measured. We want the taste of garlic to be present but not too pronounced, and found the result with 3 garlic cloves. To be more precise, we recommend using ½ oz (15 g) of garlic.

CREAMY EGG WHITES The garlic sauce's rich and creamy texture is due to using egg whites only, which also gives the sauce its characteristic white color.

CREAM-BASED MARINADE The marinade step is crucial as the chicken acquires its taste and tenderness while resting in the mixture. The cream, combined with the garlic sauce and oil, coats the meat well, all while favoring caramelization.

ON THE GRILL Given most of us don't own a spit that cooks shish taouk meat vertically, we instead cook it on the grill. We use chicken breasts; they're just thick enough that the grill temperature doesn't need to be too high, resulting in juicy, perfectly cooked meat.

Souvlaki Skewers

PREPARATION 30 minutes
MARINATING 2 hours
COOKING 15 minutes
SERVINGS 4

½ cup	(125 ml) olive oil
½ cup	(125 ml) lemon juice
2 tbsp	dried oregano
4	garlic cloves, finely grated
2¼ lb	(1 kg) boneless, skinless chicken breasts or boneless pork loin roast (from the rib end), cubed
½ tsp	salt

In a large bowl, whisk together the oil, lemon juice, oregano and garlic. Set aside ⅓ cup (75 ml) of the marinade and refrigerate until ready to use.

Add the meat and salt to the bowl with the remaining marinade. Season with pepper. Mix well. Cover and refrigerate for 2 hours.

Preheat the grill, setting the burners to high. Oil the grate.

Thread the meat onto metal or wooden skewers (if wooden, soak in water for 30 minutes before using).

Grill the meat skewers for 2 minutes on each side. Continue to grill for 6 minutes, turning the meat over a few times. Reduce the temperature of the grill. Using a pastry brush, coat the skewers with the reserved marinade. Continue to grill for 2 minutes or until the chicken is cooked through.

Serve the souvlaki skewers with rice, Tzatziki (p. 27) and grilled Greek-style pitas, if desired.

QUICK AND EASY MARINADE Only four ingredients are required for our skewer marinade: oil, garlic, oregano and lemon. We use lemon juice for its freshness rather than vinegar, which gave a bitter taste to the meat. The meat needs to be marinated for 2 to 3 hours, otherwise it may dry out. The acidity of the marinade tenderizes the meat, but can also make it tough if it sits for too long.

OREGANO FLAVOR Dried oregano often gets a bad rap, but unlike various other herbs, its flavor is much more complex and concentrated than when fresh. However, if your dried oregano has been sitting in the cupboard for a while, be sure to check that it still has its aroma before using it in a recipe, as it can lose its flavor over time.

BEST WHEN GRATED This marinade requires a good dose of garlic. To make sure it releases its full flavor, we chose to grate it rather than chop it, reducing it to a paste. This way, it coats the meat better and is less likely to burn on the grill than if it were chopped into little pieces.

INTERCHANGEABLE MEATS Souvlaki skewers can be made using either pork or chicken, depending on your preference. The same amount of marinade is used for both, and both the marinating and cooking times remain the same. However, make sure that the chicken is well cooked and that the pork is perfectly pink inside before serving.

Moussaka

PREPARATION 30 minutes
COOKING 1 hour 15 minutes
WAITING 15 minutes
SERVINGS 8
FREEZES WELL

Vegetables

1¾ lb	(800 g) white potatoes, peeled and cut into slices ⅛ inch (3 mm) thick on a mandoline (about 4 medium potatoes)
6 tbsp	(90 ml) olive oil
2	medium eggplants, cut into rounds ½ inch (1 cm) thick
2	garlic cloves, chopped
1½ tsp	dried oregano

Meat Filling

1½ lb	(675 g) ground lamb or medium-lean ground beef
1 tbsp	(15 ml) olive oil
¼ tsp	ground cinnamon
1 pinch	cayenne pepper
2	onions, chopped
2	garlic cloves, chopped
1 tbsp	(15 ml) tomato paste
2 tsp	sweet paprika
½ cup	(125 ml) dry white wine
1 can	(28 oz/796 ml) whole plum tomatoes

Béchamel

6 tbsp	(85 g) butter
½ cup	(75 g) unbleached all-purpose flour
2½ cups	(625 ml) milk
⅛ tsp	ground nutmeg
½ cup	(35 g) grated fresh Pecorino cheese
2	egg yolks

Vegetables

With one rack in the lower third and a second rack in the upper third, preheat the oven to 425°F (220°C).

In a 13 × 9-inch (33 × 23 cm) baking dish, toss the potatoes with 1 tbsp (15 ml) of the oil. Season with salt and pepper. Spread the potatoes out in the baking dish.

In a large bowl, combine the eggplants, garlic, oregano and remaining oil. Season with salt and pepper. Spread the mixture out on a non-stick or parchment paper-lined baking sheet, letting the eggplant slices overlap slightly.

Bake the potatoes on the lower rack of the oven and the eggplant on the upper rack for 30 minutes or until the eggplant slices are tender and golden and the potatoes are starting to soften. Let cool. Cover the potatoes with the eggplant mixture. Set aside. Reduce the oven temperature to 375°F (190°C).

Meat Filling

Meanwhile, in a large, deep skillet over high heat, cook the ground meat in the oil with the cinnamon and cayenne, breaking the meat up with a wooden spoon until browned, about 8 minutes. Season with salt and pepper. Drain the meat through a strainer set over a bowl. Remove 3 tbsp (45 ml) of the cooking fat from the bowl and place in the skillet.

In the same skillet over medium heat, lightly brown the onions in the cooking fat, stirring often, about 5 minutes. Add the garlic and continue to cook for 2 minutes while stirring. Add the tomato paste and paprika. Cook for 1 minute while stirring. Deglaze with the wine and let reduce until almost dry. Add the tomatoes and crush them with a wooden spoon. Return the ground meat to the skillet and mix well. Simmer for 15 minutes or until the mixture thickens. Adjust the seasoning. Spread over the eggplant layer in the baking dish.

Béchamel

In a pot over medium heat, melt the butter. Add the flour and cook for 1 minute while whisking. Whisk in the milk and nutmeg. Bring to a boil while whisking. Simmer gently for 1 minute or until the sauce thickens. Remove from the heat.

Add the Pecorino and egg yolks to the pot. Mix well. Adjust the seasoning. Pour the béchamel over the meat filling and spread out using a spatula (see note). Bake on the upper rack of the oven for 20 minutes or until the béchamel is golden. Finish off under the broiler, if desired. Let sit for 15 minutes before serving.

| NOTE | You can assemble and refrigerate the moussaka the night before you plan to cook it. In this case, add 10 to 15 minutes to the baking time.

COOK SEPARATELY To ensure the vegetables don't get too softened by the meat and the béchamel, bake them separately in the oven before assembly. This is also to make sure the eggplant is tender but not too soft, and the potatoes are al dente.

FLAVORFUL MEAT Ground lamb is typically used in a classic moussaka. Although the strong flavor of the meat enhances the dish, it can easily be replaced with ground beef. Cayenne pepper, cinnamon, paprika and white wine also give this dish plenty of depth. Add the plum tomatoes and then cook them down to reduce the mixture and keep the filling from being too liquid.

GENEROUS WHITE SAUCE The top layer of the moussaka consists of a béchamel with egg yolks, which make it rich and help it hold its shape. Freshly grated Pecorino cheese further enhances the sauce. Then place the moussaka under the broiler at the end of cooking, which gives the béchamel a light golden color.

Butter Chicken

PREPARATION 25 minutes
COOKING 30 minutes
SERVINGS 4
FREEZES WELL

Chicken

2¼ lb	(1 kg) boneless, skinless chicken thighs, cubed
½ cup	(125 ml) plain yogurt
2	garlic cloves, finely chopped
1 tbsp	finely chopped fresh ginger
1 tbsp	garam masala
½ tsp	salt
1	lime, juiced

Sauce

1	onion, chopped
1	small jalapeño chili pepper, seeded and chopped
2	garlic cloves, chopped
1 tbsp	chopped fresh ginger
3 tbsp	butter
1 tbsp	garam masala
1 tbsp	(15 ml) tomato paste
1 can	(14 oz/398 ml) diced tomatoes
½ cup	(125 ml) chicken broth
½ cup	(125 ml) 35% cream
¼ cup	(10 g) finely chopped cilantro

Chicken

With the rack in the middle position, preheat the oven to 500°F (260°C). Line a baking sheet with foil. Lightly butter the foil.

In a large bowl, combine the chicken, yogurt, garlic, ginger, garam masala, salt and lime juice. Spread the mixture out on the baking sheet. Bake for 15 minutes or until the chicken is cooked through. Set aside.

Sauce

Meanwhile, in a large pot over medium heat, lightly brown the onion, jalapeño, garlic and ginger in the butter. Add the garam masala and tomato paste. Continue to cook for 2 minutes while stirring. Add the diced tomatoes and broth. Season with salt and pepper. Simmer for 15 minutes. Add the 35% cream. Remove from the heat.

Using a hand blender, purée the sauce until smooth. Adjust the seasoning. Add the cooked chicken to the sauce and stir for a few minutes or until the sauce is very thick.

Sprinkle with the cilantro. Serve with white rice and naan bread, if desired.

CHICKEN CUTS We use chicken thighs here because they're tender and full of flavor. You can also use chicken breast, but you will have to let it marinate in the yogurt mixture for at least 30 minutes and up to 24 hours before cooking because the white meat is drier.

QUICK AND EASY GARAM MASALA In this recipe, we use a garam masala blend found in grocery stores. To make your own at home, combine 1 tbsp ground cumin, 2 tsp ground coriander, 1½ tsp ground cardamom, 1 tsp ground cinnamon, 1 tsp ground black pepper and ½ tsp ground nutmeg.

SAUCE TEXTURE A classic butter chicken calls for a creamy, homogeneous sauce, but if you're whipping this dish up on a busy weeknight and want to keep things simple, skip the step that calls for puréeing the sauce.

ALWAYS A CLASSIC Butter chicken is a long-standing favorite at RICARDO. We've got a slow cooker version, a quick and easy version, one made with tofu, one featuring 27 ingredients, and then this recipe, our best ever!

Crab Cakes

PREPARATION 25 minutes
COOKING 16 minutes
SERVINGS 4 to 6
FREEZES WELL

Crab Cakes

36	soda crackers, finely crushed (about 1½ cups)
¼ cup	(60 ml) milk
1 lb	(450 g) cooked fresh crabmeat, in large pieces, or a mixture of equal parts cooked frozen crabmeat and raw shelled and deveined shrimp, patted very dry and chopped
¼ cup	(10 g) finely chopped chives
¼ cup	(60 ml) mayonnaise
1 tbsp	butter, melted
1 tbsp	(15 ml) lemon juice
1 tsp	(5 ml) Dijon mustard
1	egg
	Hot sauce, to taste
2 tbsp	(30 ml) olive oil

Tartar Sauce

¾ cup	(180 ml) mayonnaise
¼ cup	(60 ml) sour cream
2 tbsp	finely chopped sour gherkins
1 tbsp	finely chopped parsley leaves
1 tbsp	capers, chopped
1 tbsp	finely chopped shallot
1 tsp	(5 ml) Worcestershire sauce
1 tsp	(5 ml) gherkin juice
½ tsp	(2.5 ml) prepared horseradish
	Cayenne pepper, to taste

Crab Cakes

In a large bowl, combine half of the crushed crackers with the milk. Let soak for 5 minutes. Set the remaining crushed crackers aside in a shallow bowl.

Add the crabmeat, chives, mayonnaise, butter, lemon juice, mustard, egg and hot sauce to the large bowl of soaked crackers. Mix gently to avoid breaking up the crabmeat. Season with pepper (do not add salt, as the crab is already quite salty).

Using your hands, shape the crab mixture into six patties and place on a large plate.

Lightly press the patties into the reserved crushed crackers to coat well.

In a non-stick skillet over medium-low heat, brown half of the patties at a time in the oil for 4 to 5 minutes on each side or until nicely browned. Drain on a plate lined with paper towels. Keep warm. Cook the remaining patties, adding more oil as needed.

Tartar Sauce

In a small bowl, combine all of the ingredients. Season with salt and pepper. The tartar sauce will keep for 1 week in an airtight container in the refrigerator. Serve the crab cakes with the tartar sauce.

YEAR-ROUND CRAB Given that fresh crab season is very brief, we developed a version of this recipe that could be made off season. After multiple tests, we chose cooked frozen crab combined with equal parts chopped shrimp. This provides not only the desired crab flavor, but also a firmer texture thanks to the shrimp.

CLASSIC CRUMBS When creating this recipe, the one thing we didn't want to lose sight of was the balance between the uniquely delicate crabmeat and the other ingredients. To do this, we needed to first choose the right type of crumbs for coating—ultimately, we selected crushed saltine crackers, as they best enhance the crab and provide the perfect texture. Adding the saltine coating before frying the crab cakes ensures the outside stays crispy and the inside is moist.

FRIED UNTIL CRISPY For evenly cooked crab cakes, shape them into flat patties rather than meatballs. Our reason for pan frying instead of deep frying is a practical one: we don't want to taint the frying oil with the taste of fish for just one cooking session, when it's possible to reuse that volume of oil again.

Barbecue Ribs

PREPARATION 35 minutes
MARINATING 1 hour
COOKING 2 hours 10 minutes
SERVINGS 4

Ribs

2 tbsp	brown sugar
1 tbsp	chili powder
2 tsp	salt
1 tsp	ground black pepper
1 tsp	dry mustard
½ tsp	onion powder
5 lb	(2.3 kg) baby back pork ribs

Barbecue Sauce

1 tsp	chili powder
1 tsp	onion powder
½ tsp	garlic powder
2 tbsp	butter
¾ cup	(180 ml) ketchup
¾ cup	(180 ml) apple jelly
¼ cup	(60 ml) apple cider vinegar
2 tbsp	(30 ml) molasses
1 tbsp	(15 ml) Dijon mustard
1 tbsp	(15 ml) Worcestershire sauce
	Hot sauce, to taste

Ribs

In a bowl, combine the brown sugar, chili powder, salt, pepper, mustard and onion powder.

On a work surface, using paper towels, peel away and compost the white membrane from the back of the ribs. Place the ribs on a baking sheet and sprinkle with the spice mixture, rubbing thoroughly into the meat on both sides. Cover and refrigerate for 1 hour or overnight.

With the rack in the middle position, preheat the oven to 325°F (165°C).

Wrap the ribs, two racks at a time, with foil. Place on a baking sheet. Bake for 2 hours or until the meat is tender.

Barbecue Sauce

Meanwhile, in a small pot over medium heat, cook the chili powder, onion powder and garlic powder in the butter for 1 minute. Add the ketchup, apple jelly, vinegar, molasses, mustard, Worcestershire sauce and hot sauce and bring to a boil. Simmer for 5 minutes or until the sauce is thick and syrupy. Season with salt and pepper. Remove from the heat.

Preheat the grill, setting the burners to medium. Oil the grate.

Remove the ribs from the foil. Grill for 4 to 5 minutes on each side, brushing with half of the barbecue sauce. Serve the ribs with the remaining sauce.

MORE MEAT We prefer baby back ribs over spare ribs. They're more tender, less fatty and have less cartilage, which can get chewy and rubbery. Even though they're pricier, their meat-to-fat-to-bone ratio is much better.

REMOVE THE MEMBRANE For even more delicious ribs, remove the white membrane that covers the back. Using a paper towel, pull off one end of the membrane, and it should completely and easily detach.

POACH OR BRAISE? Rather than cook the ribs using the traditional boiling water method, we prefer to wrap them in foil and braise them in the oven instead. This makes them tender without falling off the bone, and doesn't give off the same unpleasant smell that poaching does.

TWICE COOKED The rub flavors the meat as it cooks for the first time in the oven. Then the sauce adds a caramelized sweet-and-sour flavor as the ribs cook a second time on the grill.

TASTY LEFTOVERS Add a bit of sauce to your leftover ribs, cover in aluminum foil and warm them in a 250°F (120°C) oven for 1 hour. Remove the foil for the final 10 minutes.

Chili *con Carne*

PREPARATION 45 minutes
COOKING 1 hour 25 minutes
SERVINGS 8
FREEZES WELL

Chili

¼ lb	(115 g) thick bacon slices, diced
1 tbsp	(15 ml) olive oil
2 lb	(900 g) lean ground beef
2	onions, chopped
2	garlic cloves, chopped
1 tbsp	ancho chili powder or 4 tsp regular chili powder
2 tsp	sweet paprika
1½ tsp	ground cumin
1 tsp	dried oregano
½ tsp	ground black pepper
2½ cups	(625 ml) beef broth
2 cans	(19 oz/540 ml each) red kidney beans, rinsed and drained
1 can	(28 oz/796 ml) diced tomatoes

Corn Salad

1 cup	(150 g) frozen corn kernels
½ cup	(25 g) finely chopped cilantro stems and leaves
½	red bell pepper, seeded and diced
1 tbsp	(15 ml) lime juice

Marinated Red Onions

1	small red onion, thinly sliced
2 tbsp	(30 ml) lime juice
½ tsp	sugar
¼ tsp	salt

Chili

In a large pot over medium heat, brown the bacon in the oil. Using a slotted spoon, remove the bacon from the pot and drain in a bowl lined with paper towels.

In the same pot over high heat, cook the beef in the bacon fat, breaking it up with a wooden spoon until it starts to brown. Add the onions and continue to cook over medium heat for 3 minutes. Add the garlic, chili powder, paprika, cumin, oregano and pepper. Cook for 1 minute while stirring. Add the broth, beans, tomatoes and bacon. Mix well. Bring to a boil. Simmer for 50 minutes or until the chili has thickened, stirring regularly. Adjust the seasoning.

Corn Salad

Meanwhile, in a small pot of boiling salted water, cook the corn kernels for 2 minutes. Drain and let cool.

In a bowl, combine the corn with the cilantro, bell pepper and lime juice. Season with salt and pepper. Let marinate for 10 minutes.

Marinated Red Onions

Meanwhile, in another bowl, combine the onion, lime juice, sugar and salt. Let marinate for 10 minutes. Drain before serving.

Divide the chili among eight bowls. Top with the corn salad and marinated red onions. Serve with grated cheddar cheese or sour cream, if desired.

THE POWER OF BACON Bacon is the ultimate ally in this chili. Its deliciously smoky aroma gives the impression that the dish has been slow cooked over charcoal. When well incorporated, you won't bite into individual pieces of bacon, but you'll still enjoy its deep flavor throughout.

EXTRA PROTEIN As its Spanish name suggests, this chili contains a lot of meat: 2 lb (900 g) of ground beef. The beef carries the dish's hearty flavor while the spices lend it a beautiful red hue as it cooks. We also add 2 cans of red kidney beans to bulk up the chili and make it more nutritious.

PERFECTLY SPICY Our chili balances a good blend of spices to enhance flavor without making it overwhelmingly spicy. Paprika adds mild warmth, cumin deepens the taste, and a touch of dried oregano (often used in Mexican cuisine) adds its own aromatic character to the mix.

FEATURED CHILI PEPPER Ground ancho chili is our secret ingredient here. It brings some heat and a subtle fruity depth that rounds out the flavors. Mix it in with the meat as you begin cooking, just before adding the beef broth.

Barbecue Chicken Skewers

PREPARATION 20 minutes
MARINATING 24 hours
COOKING 15 minutes
SERVINGS 4

Skewers

½ cup	(125 ml) buttermilk
1 tsp	onion powder
1 tsp	garlic powder
½ tsp	ground allspice
½ tsp	cayenne pepper
1½ lb	(675 g) boneless, skinless chicken breasts, cubed
6	green onions, cut into pieces 1½ inches (4 cm) long (optional)

Barbecue Sauce

¼ cup	(60 ml) ketchup
2 tbsp	(30 ml) water
1 tbsp	(15 ml) tomato paste
1 tbsp	(15 ml) maple syrup
1 tsp	sweet paprika
½ tsp	ground coriander
¼ tsp	ground allspice
	Vegetable oil, for brushing

Skewers

In a glass dish, whisk together the buttermilk, onion powder, garlic powder, allspice and cayenne. Season with salt and pepper. Add the chicken and mix well to coat with the marinade. Cover and refrigerate for 24 hours.

Barbecue Sauce

In a glass bowl, whisk together the ketchup, water, tomato paste, maple syrup, paprika, coriander and allspice. Cook in the microwave oven for 1 minute or until the sauce is boiling. Set half of the sauce aside for serving.

Preheat the grill, setting the burners to medium. Oil the grate.

Drain the chicken and pat slightly dry. Discard the marinade. Thread the chicken cubes onto metal or wooden skewers (if wooden, soak in water for 30 minutes before using), alternating with the green onions. Place on a plate. Using a pastry brush, lightly oil the chicken skewers.

Grill the skewers for 5 minutes on each side. Brush the chicken with the remaining barbecue sauce. Continue to grill for 1 minute on each side or until the chicken is cooked through. Set aside on a clean plate and tent with foil. Let rest for 5 minutes.

Serve the skewers and the reserved barbecue sauce with rice and green salad, if desired.

BALANCED MARINADE We opt for a buttermilk marinade here with balanced acidity to give the chicken tenderness and juiciness; marinating for up to 24 hours ensures the meat stays moist. We also avoid adding too much salt, which tends to dry out the meat.

VEGGIES ON THE SIDE Where did we put the peppers, onions and other vegetables that are usually threaded on the skewers? Because vegetables don't have the same cooking time as meat, they often end up either charred or raw, so it's best to cook them separately, on skewers or in a barbecue cooking basket.

MODERATE HEAT Delicate chicken cooks best over moderate heat, even if it takes longer. To prevent dryness, remove the chicken from the grill as soon as it reaches an internal temperature of 165°F (74°C). Cover with aluminum foil and let it rest for 5 minutes to finish cooking evenly.

RED SAUCE The tangy red sauce used to glaze the chicken here adds color and brightness. Brush it on the skewers at the end of cooking to control the caramelization and then serve some extra sauce on the side for dipping. We use a simple base of ketchup and spices to create the sauce.

Paella

PREPARATION 45 minutes
COOKING 45 minutes
SERVINGS 8

4 cups	(1 L) chicken broth
3 tbsp	(45 ml) tomato paste
½ tsp	smoked paprika
2	fresh artichoke bottoms, cut into thin wedges
1 pinch	saffron
¾ lb	(340 g) boneless, skinless chicken thighs, cubed
3 tbsp	(45 ml) olive oil
1	onion, chopped
2	garlic cloves, chopped
1	red bell pepper, seeded and cut into strips
2	squid without tentacles, trimmed and cut into thin strips
5 oz	(140 g) dry chorizo sausage, sliced into rounds
1½ cups	(330 g) paella rice
½ cup	(125 ml) dry white wine
¾ lb	(340 g) large shrimp (16–20), shelled and deveined with tails intact, patted very dry
20	mussels, trimmed and washed
½ cup	(75 g) frozen green peas, thawed
	Lemon wedges, to taste

In a large pot, combine the broth, tomato paste, paprika and artichokes. Bring to a boil. Simmer for 5 minutes. Add the saffron. Season with salt and pepper. Mix well. Keep warm.

Meanwhile, in a paella pan or large non-stick skillet over high heat, brown the chicken in the oil. Add the onion and garlic. Cook for 1 minute while stirring. Add the bell pepper, squid and chorizo. Season with salt and pepper. Continue to cook for 2 minutes while stirring.

Add the rice to the pan and mix well. Add the wine and cook for 1 minute. Add the broth with the artichokes and simmer over medium heat for 10 minutes without stirring. Place the shrimp over the rice. Nestle the mussels into the rice with the openings facing up. Continue to cook for 10 to 12 minutes or until the rice is cooked but still slightly firm, the broth is thickened but not completely absorbed, and the shrimp and mussels are cooked. Remove from the heat. Discard any mussels that have not opened.

Add the peas to the pan. Cover loosely with foil and let sit for 3 minutes. Serve the paella with lemon wedges.

CHOICE OF RICE In Spain, short and round bomba rice is used for paella. Given that it may be hard to find on our side of the Atlantic Ocean, you can instead use arborio rice (also known as risotto rice). It's a porous variety of rice that can absorb the flavors of meat, seafood and spices without becoming waterlogged.

NO STIRRING The golden rule when it comes to cooking rice? Don't stir it! This is to keep the starch from releasing and the rice from getting mushy. In this recipe, leaving the rice unstirred also lets it form a lightly browned crust underneath, reminiscent of the classic wood fire method traditionally used for paella.

COOKING THE ADD-INS The squid should be included at the beginning of cooking as it needs more time to cook until tender, and it also brings flavor to the broth. Shrimp and mussels cook quickly, so those can be added to the rice halfway through.

LET IT REST Cook this recipe uncovered so that the broth evaporates, ensuring the food is coated in liquid but not swimming in it. Let the dish rest at the end of the cooking time by covering it with a sheet of aluminum foil. This allows the shrimp and mussels to finish cooking, the spice blend to develop its flavors and the peas to warm up.

Stuffed Turkey Roast

PREPARATION 45 minutes
BRINING 12 hours
COOKING 2 hours
CHILLING 30 minutes
SERVINGS 8
FREEZES WELL

Turkey

12 cups	(3 L) water
¼ cup	(60 g) salt
3 tbsp	brown sugar
1 tsp	crushed black peppercorns
2	bay leaves
1	deboned turkey roast with or without skin, about 4 lb (1.8 kg)
	Vegetable oil, for brushing

Stuffing

1	onion, finely chopped
1	garlic clove, finely chopped
¼ cup	(25 g) fresh or frozen cranberries
2 tbsp	butter
¼ lb	(115 g) lean ground pork
1	pear, cored and chopped
2 tbsp	(30 ml) fortified wine (such as port, sherry, Marsala)
¼ cup	(60 ml) chicken broth
2 tbsp	dried breadcrumbs
1 pinch	ground nutmeg

Gravy

1	onion, finely chopped
2	garlic cloves, finely chopped
2 tbsp	butter
2 tbsp	unbleached all-purpose flour
2 cups	(500 ml) chicken broth
¼ cup	(60 ml) fortified wine (such as port, sherry, Marsala)

Turkey

In a 24-cup (6 L) pot, bring 2 cups (500 ml) of the water to a boil with the salt and brown sugar, stirring until the sugar has dissolved. Remove the brine from the heat.

Add the peppercorns, bay leaves and remaining water to the brine. Place the turkey roast in the pot. Place a plate over the roast to weigh it down and to keep it completely submerged. Refrigerate for 12 hours.

Stuffing

In a skillet over medium heat, soften the onion, garlic and cranberries in half of the butter (1 tbsp) until the cranberries start to burst. Continue to cook for 1 minute. Season with salt and pepper. Transfer to a bowl.

In the same skillet, cook the pork in the remaining butter, breaking the meat up with a wooden spoon until starting to brown. Season with salt and pepper. Add the pear and continue to cook for 2 minutes. Add the fortified wine and broth. Let reduce until almost dry. Stir in the breadcrumbs and nutmeg. Adjust the seasoning. Transfer to the bowl of cranberries and mix to combine. Cover and refrigerate for 30 minutes.

With the rack in the lowest position, preheat the oven to 375°F (190°C).

Drain the turkey roast from the brine and pat dry with paper towels. On a work surface, unroll the roast and lay it flat, skin-side down. Spread the cooled stuffing over the center of the breasts and roll the roast back up.

Slide several pieces of butcher's twine under the meat, letting them extend on either side. Tie the roast and cut off any excess twine.

Place the roast in a baking dish. Using a pastry brush, lightly coat the roast with oil. Bake for 1 hour 30 minutes or until a meat thermometer inserted in the center of the stuffing reads 165°F (74°C). Add a small amount of water to the baking dish, as needed, to prevent the cooking juices from burning. Transfer the roast to a plate and let rest while you make the gravy. Set the cooking juices aside to use in the gravy.

Gravy

In a skillet over medium heat, brown the onion and garlic in the butter. Sprinkle in the flour and mix well. Add the broth, fortified wine and reserved turkey cooking juices. Bring to a boil while whisking constantly. Simmer over high heat for 10 minutes or until the gravy thickens. Adjust the seasoning. Strain through a sieve, if desired.

Remove the butcher's twine from the roast. On a work surface, slice the roast. Serve the turkey and gravy with Mashed Potatoes (p. 43) and green beans, if desired.

MUST BRINE Because a turkey roast is smaller than a whole bird, it can be fully submerged in a wet brine. The combination of water, salt, brown sugar and aromatics infuses more flavor into the poultry than a dry brine, and helps the meat retain moisture, solving the dryness challenge often associated with roasting a turkey.

SEASONAL FRUIT For the stuffing, we chose a meat base enhanced by pears and cranberries. Fresh or frozen cranberries work best since they're less sweet than their canned counterparts, giving the stuffing a balanced and tart note.

MULTIPURPOSE BREADCRUMBS Breadcrumbs allow the stuffing to absorb the fruit juices released during baking without becoming soggy. We prefer store-bought dried breadcrumbs over fresh for their even texture and consistent results.

FORTIFIED WINE To complement the turkey's delicate flavor, we developed a slightly sweet gravy enriched with fortified wine. Its gentle acidity and dose of concentrated sugars enhance the sauce perfectly. Port, sherry or Marsala all work well.

Roasted Whole Turkey with Stuffing

PREPARATION 50 minutes
MARINATING 2 days
CHILLING 2 hours
COOKING 4 hours
SERVINGS 8

Turkey

1	whole turkey, about 11 lb (5 kg)
2 tbsp	salt
2 tsp	finely chopped rosemary leaves
½ tsp	ground black pepper
½	lemon
3	slices bacon, halved
	Vegetable oil, for brushing
½ cup	(125 ml) water

Stuffing

4 cups	(200 g) diced crustless country bread
¾ lb	(340 g) lean ground pork
¾ lb	(340 g) lean ground veal
2	onions, chopped
2	celery stalks with leaves, diced
2 tbsp	butter
½ cup	(125 ml) dry white wine
2 cups	(500 ml) chicken broth
½ cup	(125 ml) unsweetened applesauce
½ tsp	ground allspice
3 tbsp	finely chopped flat-leaf parsley

Gravy

2	shallots, finely chopped
2 tbsp	butter
½ cup	(125 ml) dry white wine
2 tbsp	(30 ml) brandy (optional)
2 cans	(10 oz/284 ml each) low-sodium condensed chicken broth, undiluted
3 tbsp	lightly toasted flour
1 pinch	ground nutmeg

Turkey (2 days before serving)

Remove the bag of giblets from inside the turkey cavity, if there is one. Set aside for another use. Pat the cavity dry with paper towels.

Place the turkey in a large glass or ceramic baking dish, breast-side up.

In a small bowl, combine the salt, rosemary and black pepper. Cover the turkey skin with half of the salt mixture. Rub the salted skin as well as the cavity of the turkey with the cut-side of the lemon for 2 minutes. Sprinkle with the remaining salt mixture, focusing primarily on the breasts. Cover with plastic wrap and refrigerate for 2 days.

Stuffing

Meanwhile, with the rack in the middle position, preheat the oven to 350°F (180°C).

Spread the diced bread out on a baking sheet. Bake for 12 minutes or until dried out and golden. Set aside.

Meanwhile, in a large, deep skillet over medium-high heat, cook the pork, veal, onions and celery in the butter, breaking the meat up with a wooden spoon, for 12 minutes or until starting to brown and the liquid has completely evaporated.

Deglaze with the wine and let reduce until almost dry. Add the broth, applesauce, allspice, parsley and toasted bread. Bring to a boil. Simmer for 10 minutes or until the mixture firms up and the liquid has completely evaporated. Season with salt and pepper. Transfer to a glass dish and let cool. Cover with plastic wrap and refrigerate for 2 hours or until completely chilled. The stuffing can be made up to 2 days in advance while the turkey is marinating.

Turkey (day of serving)

With the rack in the lowest position, preheat the oven to 350°F (180°C).

Pat the turkey very dry with paper towels.

Place the turkey in a large roasting pan, breast-side up. If you have the turkey neck, place it in the roasting pan. Fill the main cavity of the turkey (between the legs) as well as the neck cavity with the stuffing. Fold the skin over the neck cavity to seal in the stuffing. Cover the stuffing in the main cavity with the bacon, letting the slices overlap slightly. Tie the legs with butcher's twine. Using a pastry brush, cover the skin with oil.

→

Bake for 3 hours or until a thermometer inserted in the thigh without touching bone reads 180°F (82°C). If the turkey is browning too quickly after the first hour of roasting, tent loosely with foil. Remove the foil during the last 30 minutes of the cooking time. Add the water to deglaze the roasting pan at the end of the cooking time. Set the turkey aside on a large plate and keep warm. Strain and remove any excess fat from the cooking juices.

Gravy

In a large skillet over medium-high heat, brown the shallots in the butter. Deglaze with the wine and brandy. Let reduce by half. Add the broth, toasted flour and nutmeg. Bring to a boil while whisking constantly. Simmer over medium heat for 5 minutes or until the gravy thickens. Pour in the turkey cooking juices and simmer until the sauce has reduced to 2 cups (500 ml). Adjust the seasoning.

Serve the turkey and gravy with vegetables and Mashed Potatoes (p. 43), if desired.

SIMPLE BRINE We preferred a dry brine over a wet version. Sprinkle salt seasoned with rosemary over the skin, and the flavor will permeate the meat subtly. Then rub the surface with half a lemon before seasoning one more time. Let time take its course, and the result is a juicy, flavorful bird.

TASTES LIKE TRADITION For the stuffing, we use a list of simple ingredients boasting nostalgic holiday flavors. To keep the exposed part of the stuffing from drying out as it bakes, cover it with slices of bacon, which also helps to enhance the taste.

ESSENTIAL STUFFING A blend of ground meat and bread in the stuffing brings flavor and moisture to the turkey, by creating a humid environment that keeps the inside from drying out in the heat. Filling the cavity gives the turkey structure and an aesthetically pleasing look, as it wouldn't look as rounded coming out of the oven without the stuffing.

AN EYE ON THE CLOCK Roasting time is 3 hours, but it's still important to check the turkey's internal temperature with a thermometer to make sure it's fully cooked. A long and stable roast is preferable to one that starts out at a high temperature, and potentially blackens the skin.

SUCCULENT SAUCE The secret to a tasty sauce is saving the pan drippings from the turkey by deglazing the roasting pan with water, then adding the drippings to the skillet once the sauce has been thickened with the chicken broth and toasted flour. Simmer and reduce the sauce for more intense flavor.

The Best Desserts

Chewy Chocolate Chip Cookies

PREPARATION 15 minutes
CHILLING 1 hour
COOKING 8 minutes per batch
MAKES 16
FREEZES WELL

1½ cups	(225 g) unbleached all-purpose flour
½ tsp	baking soda
1 pinch	salt
¾ cup	(170 g) unsalted butter, melted and cooled
1 cup	(210 g) brown sugar
2 tbsp	sugar
1	egg
1	egg yolk
7 oz	(200 g) milk or dark chocolate, coarsely chopped

In a bowl, combine the flour, baking soda and salt.

In another bowl, combine the melted butter and both sugars with a wooden spoon. Add the egg and egg yolk. Mix until smooth. Stir in the dry ingredients and chocolate. Cover and refrigerate for 1 hour or overnight.

With the rack in the middle position, preheat the oven to 375°F (190°C). Line two baking sheets with silicone mats or parchment paper.

Using a 3-tbsp (45 ml) ice cream scoop, shape the mixture into balls. Freeze some or all of the cookies at this point, if desired, evenly spaced out over one or two baking sheets (see note).

If baking right away, place 5 to 6 balls on each baking sheet, evenly spaced out. Bake one sheet at a time for 8 to 9 minutes or until golden around the edges but still very soft at the center (see note). Let cool completely on the baking sheet.

| NOTES | Once the balls of raw cookie dough are frozen, transfer them to an airtight container. They will keep for 3 months in the freezer. Before baking, let them sit out on a baking sheet at room temperature for 30 minutes. Add 2 minutes to the baking time for a total of 10 to 11 minutes.

Do not bake more than one sheet of cookies at a time, even if you rotate the baking sheets halfway through cooking.

ELEVATED FLAVORS Salt in a sweet recipe? Absolutely! It enhances the flavor of the cookies, bringing out the taste of ingredients like chocolate, vanilla and butter. If you use salted or semi-salted butter though, you can omit the added salt. Baking soda, for its part, deepens the cookies' flavor and promotes caramelization and browning, giving them a perfectly golden color.

SOFT TRIO Three ingredients bring a soft, chewy texture to these cookies: an extra egg yolk added to a whole egg, more brown sugar than regular sugar and butter melted before being added to the other ingredients.

RESTING TIME Let the dough rest for between 1 hour and 24 hours in the refrigerator to firm up. Chilled dough won't spread as much during baking and will ensure a plump cookie rather than a cracked one. Plus, the flavor becomes richer and more caramelized.

EVEN BAKING Divide the cookies between two baking sheets, but bake only one sheet at a time, placed in the center of the oven for even baking. Keep a close eye as the cookies bake, as the time can vary from one oven and batch of cookies to another, and even a single extra minute could lead to overbaked cookies. You want them to still be very soft in the middle.

Oatmeal Cookies

PREPARATION 25 minutes
COOKING 10 minutes per batch
MAKES 17
FREEZES WELL

2 cups	(300 g) unbleached all-purpose flour
2½ cups	(250 g) quick cook oats
1 tsp	baking soda
½ tsp	baking powder
½ tsp	salt
1 cup	(225 g) unsalted butter, softened
1½ cups	(315 g) brown sugar
2	eggs

With the rack in the middle position, preheat the oven to 350°F (180°C). Line two baking sheets with silicone mats or parchment paper.

In a bowl, combine the flour, oats, baking soda, baking powder and salt.

In another bowl, cream the butter and brown sugar with an electric mixer. Add the eggs and mix until smooth. With the machine running on low speed or with a wooden spoon, stir in the dry ingredients.

Using a ¼-cup (60 ml) ice cream scoop, shape the mixture into balls. If baking right away, place 5 to 6 balls on each baking sheet, evenly spaced out. Press on the balls with your hands until they are about ¾ inch (2 cm) thick. Freeze some or all of the cookies at this point, if desired, evenly spaced out over one or two baking sheets (see note).

Bake one sheet at a time for 10 to 12 minutes or until the cookies are golden. Let cool on a wire rack. Serve warm or cooled. The cookies will keep for 3 days in an airtight container at room temperature.

| NOTE | Once the balls of raw cookie dough are frozen, transfer them to an airtight container. They will keep for 3 months in the freezer. You can bake them from frozen by adding 2 minutes to the cooking time for a total of 12 to 14 minutes.

PERFECTLY SOFT The secret to a cookie that's soft on the inside and crisp on the outside? Quick cook oats so they're not too tough when you bite into them, and butter for a soft texture that lasts. Brown sugar also adds moisture. For chewier cookies, bake for slightly less time than recommended; for crispier ones, add a few extra minutes and bake until golden.

OATS AND SUGAR We use more oats than sugar in these cookies. This ratio creates a cookie that's not mealy but is bursting with the flavor of oats. And though sugar adds great sweetness to an oatmeal cookie, we reduced the amount that you'd expect to see here without affecting its taste or texture.

WINNING TRIO Baking powder is imperative, as it helps with caramelization and enhances the cookie's toasty flavor. While some recipes use oil as the fat, we like butter for the depth it imparts to the dough. A touch of salt brings out the flavors beautifully.

Maple Pudding Cake (Pouding Chômeur)

PREPARATION 20 minutes
COOKING 55 minutes
SERVINGS 8
FREEZES WELL

Sauce

1 cup	(210 g) brown sugar
4 tsp	cornstarch
1 cup	(250 ml) 35% cream
1 cup	(250 ml) maple syrup
1 cup	(250 ml) water
1 pinch	salt

Cake

1 cup	(150 g) unbleached all-purpose flour
1½ tsp	baking powder
¼ tsp	salt
½ cup	(105 g) sugar
⅓ cup	(75 g) unsalted butter, melted
1 tsp	(5 ml) vanilla
1	egg
½ cup	(125 ml) milk

Sauce

With the rack in the middle position, preheat the oven to 350°F (180°C). Place an 8-inch (20 cm) square pan on a baking sheet.

In a pot off the heat, whisk together the brown sugar and cornstarch. Add the 35% cream, maple syrup, water and salt and mix well. Bring to a boil while whisking. Simmer for 30 seconds. Pour the sauce into the pan. Set aside.

Cake

In a bowl, combine the flour, baking powder and salt.

In another bowl, whisk together the sugar, melted butter, vanilla and egg until smooth. Stir in the dry ingredients alternating with the milk. Spoon the batter over the sauce in the pan.

Bake for 45 to 50 minutes or until a toothpick inserted in the center of the cake comes out clean. Let cool on a wire rack.

A THIN SAUCE Because this cake tends to soak up moisture, you'll need a sauce that remains thin and pourable. We found the perfect mix of water, cream, maple syrup and cornstarch for a texture that's just slightly thick. The proportions in this recipe yield the best results.

IN THE POT For the right texture, we warm the sauce in a pot. The starch begins to thicken as it is heated and then the mixture cools to an ideal temperature, warm but not hot, so it doesn't congeal when the batter is poured over it.

BROWN SUGAR OR MAPLE SYRUP? We love both, so we use equal parts in the sauce. Combined with the cream and water, the final result is wonderfully balanced.

GET SAUCY One might think that a dense cake would be best here, as you find in many pudding cake recipes, but we prefer a lighter cake base for a higher sauce-to-batter ratio. Using a small amount of flour (1 cup), with butter and milk, results in a soft batter that can be spooned into the pan and baked up golden and lightly crisp on top.

Vanilla Ice Cream

PREPARATION 15 minutes
COOKING 15 minutes
CHILLING 4 hours
CHURNING 20 minutes
FREEZING 1 hour
MAKES 4 cups (1 L)

¾ cup	(160 g) sugar
1 tbsp	cornstarch
4	egg yolks
½	vanilla bean, split lengthwise and seeds scraped
1½ cups	(375 ml) 35% cream, warmed
1½ cups	(375 ml) milk, warmed

In a pot off the heat, whisk together the sugar and cornstarch. Whisk in the egg yolks, vanilla seeds and pod until smooth. Whisk in the 35% cream and milk.

Cook over medium heat, stirring constantly with a wooden spoon and scraping the bottom and sides of the pot, until the mixture begins to simmer and thickens enough to coat the back of the spoon, about 15 minutes.

Transfer to a bowl. Cover with plastic wrap directly on the surface of the mixture and let cool. Refrigerate for 4 hours or place the bowl over an ice bath for faster chilling. Strain the mixture through a sieve set over a bowl. Compost the vanilla pod (see note).

Pour the chilled mixture into an ice cream maker. Churn for 20 minutes or according to the manufacturer's instructions or until the ice cream has set.

Transfer to an airtight container. Freeze for 1 hour or until the ice cream is very firm. Let sit out at room temperature for a few minutes before serving as needed.

| NOTE | **The mixture can be made in advance and refrigerated for up to 4 days before being churned.**

SWEET ENOUGH The amount of sugar greatly affects an ice cream's texture. The more sugar, the softer and creamier it'll be; the less sugar, the firmer it becomes. After many tests, we settled on ¾ cup of sugar for the perfect softness. Any more and the ice cream would be overly sweet.

VANILLA INFUSION To ensure the vanilla flavor is fully present, we infuse the pod and seeds in the cream for over 4 hours total, from the start of cooking until just before straining. Then, once cooled, we pour the mixture through a sieve for a smooth and fragrant base.

CORNSTARCH It's our anti-curdling ally. It prevents the eggs from coagulating during the cooking process and keeps the mixture smooth from the start. Over the long term (the ice cream keeps for up to 3 weeks), it also helps prevent ice crystals from forming prematurely.

ICE CREAM MAKER A MUST An ice cream maker is essential for smooth and creamy results. It freezes the mixture while continuously stirring it. Churn the ice cream for as little time as possible to keep it from reaching a whipped texture. It's also best to pour the mixture into the machine while it's very cold; the faster it freezes, the smaller and less noticeable the crystals will be.

Date Squares

PREPARATION 20 minutes
COOKING 1 hour 5 minutes
COOLING 4 hours
MAKES 16 squares
FREEZES WELL

Filling

2½ cups	(425 g) pitted and chopped Medjool dates
1 cup	(250 ml) water
2 tbsp	(30 ml) lemon juice
2 tbsp	brown sugar
½ tsp	baking soda

Topping

1¾ cups	(175 g) quick cook oats
1 cup	(150 g) unbleached all-purpose flour
¾ cup	(160 g) brown sugar
¼ tsp	baking powder
¾ cup	(170 g) semi-salted butter, softened

Filling

With the rack in the middle position, preheat the oven to 350°F (180°C). Butter an 8-inch (20 cm) square pan and line with a strip of parchment paper, letting it hang over two sides.

In a pot, bring the dates, water, lemon juice and brown sugar to a boil. Add the baking soda and simmer for 5 minutes or until the dates have reduced to a purée, stirring constantly with a wooden spoon. Let cool.

Topping

In a bowl, combine the oats, flour, brown sugar and baking powder. Add the butter and mix well to combine.

Spread half the topping mixture out in the prepared pan, pressing down firmly. Cover with the date mixture. Finish with the remaining topping mixture, pressing down lightly.

Bake for 55 minutes or until the topping is nicely browned. Let cool on a wire rack for 4 hours.

Unmold. On a work surface, cut into squares. The date squares will keep for 1 week in an airtight container at room temperature.

FIRST MATTER We don't add a lot of sugar to this recipe, as we really want to highlight the taste of the dates. We call for large Medjool dates because they're plump, soft and tasty. They have a natural sweetness reminiscent of maple syrup and make for a smooth and dense filling. You can also use Jaffa dates, but they're grainier and more fibrous than the Medjool so your filling's texture will reflect that.

ENHANCE THE TASTE Adding a small amount of lemon juice to these squares makes a big difference, as it helps to enhance the natural flavor of the dates.

ESSENTIAL TOPPING A combination of oats, flour and brown sugar, along with some baking powder, pairs nicely with the date filling. We use quick cook oats as they're softer to bite into once baked. We also recommend semi-salted butter for a lightly salty touch, to help balance the natural sweetness of the dates.

CRISPY AND CRUNCHY When combining the ingredients for the topping, take the time to properly rub in the butter so you aren't left with a powdery texture. That way, the butter is evenly distributed among the flour and oats, ensuring a perfectly crispy layer that holds well and won't fall apart when cut into. For clean edges, let cool completely before cutting.

Lemon Poppy Seed Loaf

PREPARATION 25 minutes
COOKING 1 hour
COOLING 3 hours
SERVINGS 10
FREEZES WELL (WITHOUT THE GLAZE)

Lemon Loaf

1¾ cups	(265 g) unbleached all-purpose flour
1 tbsp	poppy seeds
2 tsp	baking powder
½ cup	(115 g) unsalted butter, softened
1¼ cups	(265 g) sugar
3	lemons, zest finely grated
3	eggs
½ cup	(125 ml) lemon juice
¼ cup	(60 ml) milk

Lemon Glaze

1 cup	(130 g) icing sugar
2 tbsp	(30 ml) lemon juice

Lemon Loaf

With the rack in the middle position, preheat the oven to 350°F (180°C). Butter a 9 × 5-inch (23 × 13 cm), 6-cup (1.5 L) loaf pan and line with a strip of parchment paper, letting it hang over two sides.

In a bowl, combine the flour, poppy seeds and baking powder.

In another bowl, cream the butter, sugar and lemon zest with an electric mixer. Add the eggs and whisk until smooth. Stir in the dry ingredients alternating with the lemon juice and milk. Pour the batter into the prepared pan.

Bake for 1 hour or until a toothpick inserted in the center of the cake comes out clean. Let cool completely on a wire rack before unmolding, about 3 hours. Freeze at this point, if desired.

Lemon Glaze

In a bowl, combine the icing sugar and lemon juice until smooth. Place the lemon poppy seed loaf on a serving dish and drizzle with the glaze.

DOUBLE DOSE OF CITRUS A great lemon loaf needs plenty of lemon flavor in the batter. For this version, we used the zest of 3 whole lemons and a generous ½ cup (125 ml) of lemon juice. Much more and the cake won't bake properly.

FRESH POPPY SEEDS You may not think about it often, but like nuts, poppy seeds can go rancid. Always check for freshness: stale seeds have a clay-like or wet cardboard taste.

CREAM GENTLY Cream the butter and sugar with the lemon zest just until the mixture thins and the sugar begins to dissolve. Doing this helps release the lemons' essential oils and ensures a homogeneous texture.

LEMONY GLAZE A simple glaze made from lemon juice and icing sugar adds a bright burst of tanginess to each bite of this loaf. Just these two ingredients are enough to create a pure lemon taste that perfectly echoes the freshness of the loaf.

Chocolate-Hazelnut Brownies

PREPARATION 20 minutes
COOKING 35 minutes
COOLING 2 hours
MAKES 16
FREEZES WELL

½ cup	(75 g) unbleached all-purpose flour
¼ tsp	salt
2	eggs
1 cup	(250 ml) chocolate-hazelnut spread
½ cup	(105 g) brown sugar
1 tsp	(5 ml) vanilla
½ cup	(115 g) unsalted butter, melted and cooled

With the rack in the middle position, preheat the oven to 325°F (165°C). Butter an 8-inch (20 cm) square pan and line with a strip of parchment paper, letting it hang over two sides.

In a bowl, combine the flour and salt.

In another bowl, whisk the eggs, chocolate-hazelnut spread, brown sugar and vanilla with an electric mixer for 2 minutes or until smooth. With the machine running on low speed, stir in the dry ingredients alternating with the melted butter. Spread the batter out in the prepared pan.

Bake for 35 to 40 minutes or until a toothpick inserted in the center of the cake comes out with a few crumbs attached and not completely clean. Let cool in the pan, about 2 hours.

Unmold. On a work surface, cut into 16 squares. Serve warm or cooled. The brownies will keep for 5 days in an airtight container at room temperature.

A HUGE SUCCESS These dessert squares weren't initially meant to be a best-ever recipe. They simply became one over time after a steady stream of glowing online reviews. In fact, over the course of 20 years, they've earned their place as one of our most beloved RICARDO classics of all time.

CHOCOLATY SPREAD To achieve a soft, fudgy texture, we use store-bought chocolate-hazelnut spread. Its sugar, cocoa and oil content help keep the brownies rich and moist, with an intense chocolate and hazelnut flavor that only deepens as they cool.

PERFECT TEXTURE Whisk the batter only until smooth and homogeneous. Overmixing adds air, causing the brownies to rise too much and lose their signature density. A gentle hand ensures a tender, fudgy treat.

CONTROLLED BAKING Given that oven intensity varies from one model to the next, it's hard to determine the perfect temperature and precise baking time for foolproof brownies. You know they're overbaked if the texture is dry and the middle is no longer gooey. We recommend removing them from the oven the moment they start to crinkle at the edges, even if they may still look wet in the center.

Apple Crisp

PREPARATION 30 minutes
COOKING 50 minutes
COOLING 1 hour
SERVINGS 10
FREEZES WELL

1 lb	(450 g) Cortland apples, peeled, cored and diced (about 4 medium apples)
1 lb	(450 g) McIntosh apples, peeled, cored and thinly sliced (about 4 medium apples)
¾ cup	(160 g) brown sugar
½ cup	(115 g) unsalted butter, softened
½ cup	(75 g) unbleached all-purpose flour
½ cup	(50 g) quick cook oats
¼ cup	(25 g) old-fashioned/large flake oats
⅛ tsp	salt

With the rack in the middle position, preheat the oven to 350°F (180°C). Butter an 8-inch (20 cm) square pan.

In a bowl, combine all of the apples with ¼ cup (55 g) of the brown sugar. Spread out in the prepared pan.

In the same bowl, combine the remaining brown sugar with the butter, flour, quick cook oats, old-fashioned oats and the salt just until the dry ingredients are moistened and the mixture comes together when pressed between your fingertips. Spread over the apples in the pan.

Bake for 50 minutes or until the oat topping is golden and the apples are cooked through. Let cool for 1 hour before serving.

| NOTE | If freezing the cooked apple crisp, let thaw in the refrigerator. Reheat the crisp on the middle rack of an oven preheated to 350°F (180°C) for 10 to 15 minutes or until heated through to the center.

GOOD APPLES The key to this recipe is the perfect mix of sweet and tart apples to create a balanced bite that's full of flavor without added sugar or lemon juice. We love using equal parts Cortland and McIntosh apples.

CHOPPING FOR TEXTURE Some people prefer apple slices, while others go for diced. We tested both and found that the former tends to break down while the latter stays intact. So we decided to use both for this crisp to achieve the best balance between soft filling and toothsome apple texture.

BACK TO BASICS To make the ultimate crumble, all you need is apples, brown sugar, butter and oats. We leave the nuts and spices behind in the pantry, preferring to add body to the crumble by combining two kinds of oats: quick cook for their flaky side and large flakes for crunch.

PERFECT SQUARE In this recipe, the size of the baking dish makes a difference: A smaller dish keeps the crumble moist, while a large one allows water to evaporate, drying it out. We recommend an 8-inch (20 cm) square pan, for the perfect crisp-to-soft ratio that tastes even better the next day.

RICARDO
0:30
Power
Low
High
Warm
Mode
Cancel
Annuler

Slow Cooker Chocolate Pudding Cake

PREPARATION 30 minutes
COOKING 2 hours
WAITING 15 minutes
SERVINGS 8

Sauce

2¼ cups	(475 g) brown sugar
½ cup	(50 g) cocoa powder
1 tbsp	cornstarch
4 oz	(115 g) 55% to 65% dark chocolate, coarsely chopped
1½ cups	(375 ml) water
1½ cups	(375 ml) 35% cream or 15% cooking cream
½ tsp	(2.5 ml) vanilla

Cake

1½ cups	(225 g) unbleached all-purpose flour
½ tsp	baking powder
½ tsp	baking soda
1 pinch	salt
¾ cup	(170 g) unsalted butter, softened
1 cup	(210 g) sugar
⅓ cup	(35 g) cocoa powder, sifted
1	egg
1	egg yolk
¾ cup	(180 ml) milk

Sauce

In a pot off the heat, whisk together the brown sugar, cocoa powder and cornstarch. Add the chocolate, water, 35% cream and vanilla. Bring to a boil while whisking. Simmer for 10 seconds. Transfer to a slow cooker.

Cake

In a bowl, combine the flour, baking powder, baking soda and salt.

In another bowl, cream the butter, sugar and cocoa powder with an electric mixer. Add the egg and egg yolk. Mix until smooth. With the machine running on low speed, stir in the dry ingredients alternating with the milk. Using an ice cream scoop or large spoon, drop the cake batter over the warm chocolate sauce in the slow cooker.

Place a clean kitchen towel over the slow cooker container, making sure it does not touch the cake batter. Cover with the lid to hold the kitchen towel in place. This will prevent water from settling on the surface of the cake.

Cook on High for 2 hours. Remove the slow cooker container. Remove the lid and kitchen towel. Let the cake sit for 15 minutes. Serve hot or cooled. Reheat the cake as needed.

SLOW COOKER We choose to use the slow cooker method for this recipe because of the steam it creates. Place a clean kitchen towel across the top to help control the moisture inside. Cook for 2 hours and you'll have a cake that's rich and soft.

COOKING CREAM Even though we love the effect that cream brings to the sauce, we wanted to steer clear of a ganache, to avoid having a sauce that is too rich or thick. We therefore use water and cream, which makes for a thin and pourable sauce. Milk instead of cream was never an option, as it would've made the sauce curdle.

TWICE THE CHOCOLATE We prepare the sauce separately here, to make sure it is homogeneous before transferring it to the slow cooker. For a tasty and creamy sauce, use a good amount of cocoa powder along with plenty of dark chocolate. The latter must contain between 55% and 65% cacao to keep bitterness in the sauce at a minimum.

SIMPLE BATTER For even more chocolate flavor, we have a simple cake batter with cocoa powder and butter. This results in a soft cake that soaks up the chocolate sauce.

Tiramisu

PREPARATION 45 minutes
COOKING 5 minutes
CHILLING 4 hours
SERVINGS 10 to 12

¾ cup	(180 ml) espresso or strong coffee, hot
1 cup	(210 g) sugar
¼ cup	(60 ml) milk
2 tbsp	(30 ml) coffee liqueur
5	egg yolks
½ tsp	(2.5 ml) vanilla
1	container (17 to 18 oz/ 475 to 500 g) mascarpone cheese
1½ cups	(375 ml) 35% whipping cream
30	ladyfingers (see note)
2 tbsp	cocoa powder, sifted

In a small bowl, combine the coffee with 2 tbsp of the sugar. Stir in the milk and coffee liqueur. Refrigerate until ready to assemble the tiramisu.

In a bowl, whisk together the egg yolks, vanilla and ¼ cup (55 g) of the sugar. Place the bowl over a pot of simmering water. Whisk continuously until the mixture forms a ribbon as it falls from the whisk, about 5 minutes. Remove the bowl from the pot. Continue to whisk with an electric mixer to cool the mixture until just slightly warm. Stir in the mascarpone.

In another bowl, whisk the 35% cream and remaining sugar with an electric mixer until stiff peaks form. Using a spatula, gently fold the whipped cream into the mascarpone mixture.

Cover the bottom of an 11 × 8-inch (28 × 20 cm), 10-cup (2.5 L) rectangular dish with a layer of ladyfingers, first dipping them in the espresso mixture for 2 to 3 seconds each. Break the ladyfingers, as needed, to make them fit. Cover with half of the mascarpone mixture. Sprinkle with half of the cocoa powder. Repeat with the remaining ingredients, ending with the cocoa powder. Cover with plastic wrap and refrigerate for 4 hours or preferably overnight.

| NOTE | Depending on the size of your dish and of your ladyfingers, you might need a few more cookies.

COFFEE LIQUEUR Rum, Marsala, amaretto, Tia Maria: we tested all four. Our search ended with Tia Maria. This coffee liqueur enhances the coffee flavor already found in the tiramisu. If you don't have any on hand, use the coffee liqueur of your choice.

CREAMY TEXTURE Classic tiramisu contains raw eggs. Since that doesn't appeal to everyone, we developed our filling using cooked eggs, which happily yields even smoother results than the original! And by using only yolks, the texture is infinitely richer.

SOAK THOSE COOKIES We have never doubted the importance of ladyfingers in this recipe. Our main concern has been how long to dunk them in coffee to ensure the tiramisu was perfectly soaked. We've found 2 or 3 seconds is enough; any more and the dessert will get soggy. For best results, add milk to the espresso.

CHOCOLATY FLAVOR We recommend sprinkling cocoa powder on each layer of this dessert, not only on top. It's the best way to bring out that chocolate flavor. The best time to do so is before you put the tiramisu in the fridge; this will bring out its full flavor.

Maple Syrup Pie

PREPARATION 25 minutes
CHILLING 30 minutes
COOKING 45 minutes
WAITING 2 hours
SERVINGS 8
FREEZES WELL

Crust

1¼ cups	(190 g) unbleached all-purpose flour
½ tsp	baking powder
¼ tsp	salt
½ cup	(115 g) cold unsalted butter, diced
3 tbsp	(45 ml) ice water

Filling

2 tbsp	cornstarch
2 tbsp	unbleached all-purpose flour
1½ cups	(375 ml) amber maple syrup
½ cup	(125 ml) 35% cream
1	egg

Crust

In a food processor, blend the flour, baking powder and salt. Add the butter and pulse a few times, until it forms pea-sized pieces. Add the water. Pulse just until the dough starts coming together. Add more water as needed. Remove the dough from the food processor and shape into a disc with your hands.

On a floured work surface, roll the dough into a circle about ⅛ inch (3 mm) thick. Line a 9-inch (23 cm) glass pie dish with the dough. Remove the excess dough hanging over the edge of the pie dish, leaving a ½-inch (1 cm) border all the way around. Tuck the border of dough under itself to form a thick crust. With your fingers, crimp the dough in a series of curves to make a decorative pattern. Refrigerate for 30 minutes.

Filling

With the rack in the lowest position, preheat the oven to 400°F (200°C).

In a bowl, whisk together the cornstarch and flour. Add the maple syrup and whisk until smooth. Stir in the 35% cream and egg. Pour into the chilled dough-lined pie dish.

Bake for 45 minutes or until the filling has set. Let cool at room temperature for 2 hours before serving. The pie will keep for 3 days, covered, in the refrigerator. Serve at room temperature or cold.

FLAKY CRUST Fashioning a flaky pie crust is no simple feat. We add a small amount of baking powder for light-as-air results. It's a little trick that makes the job easier.

TEXTURE AND TASTE To get creamy, and not runny, results every time, 1 egg is enough; more than that and the egg taste will take over. Cream gives the mixture a smooth richness, but adding too much will mask the maple. For intensely caramelized flavor, choose an amber maple syrup.

UPPER GLASS Glass pie dishes are ideal for baking sugar pies because they distribute heat well, making it easier to achieve a lovely golden-brown crust. We bake our pie at the bottom of the oven at a high temperature, which results in a perfectly set filling without leaving the crust soggy.

BAKING MADE EASY Some recipes call for the filling to be cooked on the stove and then added to a pre-baked pie crust. To save a couple of steps, we decided to cook both at the same time, which turned out to be a good idea. In addition to making the filling smoother, baking the whole pie in the oven gave the surface a nice caramelized finish.

Vanilla Cake

PREPARATION 30 minutes
COOKING 50 minutes
COOLING 2 hours
SERVINGS 12
FREEZES WELL

2⅔ cups	(400 g) unbleached all-purpose flour
2 tsp	baking powder
½ tsp	baking soda
½ tsp	salt
3	eggs
2 cups	(420 g) sugar
1 tbsp	(15 ml) vanilla
¾ cup	(180 ml) vegetable oil
1¼ cups	(310 ml) buttermilk (see note)

With the rack in the middle position, preheat the oven to 350°F (180°C). Line the bottoms of two 8-inch (20 cm) springform pans with parchment paper. Do not butter the pans.

In a bowl, combine the flour, baking powder, baking soda and salt. Set aside.

In another bowl, whisk the eggs, sugar and vanilla with an electric mixer for 5 minutes or until the mixture is pale, tripled in volume and falls from the beaters in a ribbon (using a stand mixer is preferable). Drizzle in the oil while whisking.

With the machine running on low speed, add the dry ingredients alternating with the buttermilk until the mixture is smooth. Divide the batter between the prepared pans.

Bake for 50 minutes or until a toothpick inserted in the center of a cake comes out clean. Let cool completely on a wire rack, about 2 hours, before unmolding.

Cut off the rounded top of each cake, as needed, to make them as flat as possible. Cover with Vanilla Frosting (p. 183), if desired.

| NOTE | The buttermilk can be replaced with 1¼ cups (310 ml) milk mixed with 1 tbsp (15 ml) white vinegar or lemon juice. Let sit for 5 to 10 minutes. Stir before adding to the recipe.

THE RIGHT FATS To hold together well, a cake needs fat, such as eggs, and especially butter or oil. Which should you choose? Tests showed that oil makes for a softer crumb, so we use that for the cake and butter in the frosting for flavor.

TWO MIRACLE INGREDIENTS Mixing baking soda together with buttermilk creates a chemical reaction. This makes a cake that stays moist longer and also adds a touch of tanginess, which helps to balance the flavors.

GOOD VOLUME The imposing dimensions of this cake are thanks to the baking powder, which does its job as leavening agent, as well as the eggs beaten to the ribbon stage, which bring volume to the batter. The ribbon stage is the stage when the eggs are smooth and thick, so when you lift the beaters from the bowl, the mixture falls back in a long, continuous ribbon.

VANILLA: BEAN OR EXTRACT? For recipes like crème brûlée or pastry cream, in which the flavor and delicate aroma of the vanilla is infused, it's worth paying extra for real vanilla bean. In a cake, however, given that the subtlety of the vanilla bean will be hardly noticeable, we chose the more affordable extract instead.

Vanilla Frosting

PREPARATION 20 minutes
COOKING 5 minutes
COOLING 2 hours
MAKES 4 cups (1 L), enough for a two-layer 8-inch (20 cm) cake

1½ cups	**(340 g) unsalted butter, softened**
⅓ cup	**(50 g) unbleached all-purpose flour**
1 cup	**(250 ml) milk**
¼	**vanilla bean, split lengthwise and seeds scraped, or ½ tsp (2.5 ml) vanilla**
1¼ cups	**(265 g) sugar**

In a pot, melt 1/4 cup (55 g) of the butter. Add the flour and cook for 1 minute while whisking. Add the milk and vanilla seeds. Bring to a boil while whisking. Simmer gently for 1 minute.

Transfer the mixture to a bowl. Cover with plastic wrap directly on the surface to prevent a crust from forming. Let cool for 2 hours at room temperature.

Add the sugar and remaining butter to the bowl of cooled milk mixture. Whisk with an electric mixer for 5 minutes or until the frosting is smooth and creamy (you should no longer feel any sugar crystals). Using a spatula, scrape down the sides and bottom of the bowl as needed. The frosting will keep for 3 days in an airtight container at room temperature or in the refrigerator. If refrigerated, let the frosting sit out at room temperature and whisk again until smooth and creamy before using.

To vary the flavor of the frosting, replace the milk and vanilla:

Coffee Frosting: 1 cup (250 ml) cold strong coffee

Raspberry Frosting: 1 cup (250 ml) seedless raspberry purée

Coconut Frosting: 1 cup (250 ml) coconut milk

Lemon Frosting: ½ cup (125 ml) lemon juice, ½ cup (125 ml) water and 1 egg yolk

BÉCHAMEL FROSTING Yes, the base of this ermine frosting is a béchamel, using the same base ingredients as that famous sauce: melted butter, flour and milk. This makes for a solid icing base that's extremely smooth and not too sweet.

GRANULATED OR ICING SUGAR? Unlike other frosting recipes that require icing sugar, we prefer regular white granulated sugar here. Why? Icing sugar can give a grainy texture to frosting, while granulated sugar gives one that is very creamy.

KEEP IT SIMPLE This recipe is easy to make, but it's important to follow the instructions. It's particularly imperative to let your béchamel get to room temperature. If you put it in the refrigerator, it'll get too cold and dense, making it difficult to incorporate the softened butter.

ALWAYS CREAMY We enjoy this frosting because it's smooth, multipurpose, easy to make and stable. If it's been chilled, let it get to room temperature and whip until creamy before use. You can add flavors or colors as desired using store-bought food coloring or gel paste.

Coconut Cream Pie

PREPARATION 40 minutes
COOKING 40 minutes
COOLING 5 hours
SERVINGS 8

Crust

1¼ cups	(190 g) unbleached all-purpose flour
¼ tsp	salt
½ cup	(115 g) cold unsalted butter, diced
¼ cup	(60 ml) ice water

Filling

½ cup	(105 g) sugar
3 tbsp	cornstarch
2 tbsp	unbleached all-purpose flour
2	eggs
1 can	(14 oz/398 ml) coconut milk
1 cup	(250 ml) milk
1 cup	+ 2 tbsp (130 g) sweetened shredded coconut
1 tsp	(5 ml) vanilla

Whipped Cream

1¼ cups	(310 ml) 35% whipping cream
1 tbsp	icing sugar
½ tsp	(2.5 ml) vanilla

Crust

In a food processor, blend the flour and salt. Add the butter and pulse a few times, until it forms pea-sized pieces. Add the water. Pulse just until the dough starts coming together. Add more water as needed. Remove the dough from the food processor and shape into a disc with your hands.

On a floured work surface, roll the dough into a circle about ⅛ inch (3 mm) thick. Line a 9-inch (23 cm) glass pie dish with the dough. Remove the excess dough hanging over the edge of the pie dish, leaving a ½-inch (1 cm) border all the way around. Tuck the border of dough under itself to form a thick crust. With your fingers, crimp the dough in a series of curves to make a decorative pattern. Refrigerate for 30 minutes.

With the rack in the middle position, preheat the oven to 375°F (190°C). Prick the dough with a fork. Cover the dough with foil and fill with dried beans or ceramic pie weights.

Bake for 18 minutes. Remove the pie weights and foil. Continue to bake the dough for 15 minutes or until golden. Let cool completely on a wire rack, about 30 minutes.

Filling

In a small pot off the heat, whisk together the sugar, cornstarch and flour. Add the eggs and mix well. Stir in the coconut milk, milk, 1 cup (120 g) of the shredded coconut and the vanilla. Bring to a boil over medium heat, stirring constantly and scraping the bottom and sides of the pot, until the mixture thickens. Pour into the cooled crust.

Cover with plastic wrap directly on the surface of the filling. Let cool. Refrigerate for 4 hours or until the filling has completely chilled.

Meanwhile, in a small skillet, toast the remaining coconut, stirring for 2 minutes or until golden. Transfer to a small bowl and let cool completely.

Whipped Cream

In a bowl, whisk the 35% cream, icing sugar and vanilla with an electric mixer until stiff peaks form. Garnish the pie with the whipped cream and sprinkle with the toasted coconut. The pie will keep for 3 days, covered, in the refrigerator.

GRAHAM CRACKERS OR SHORTCRUST PASTRY? Banana cream and key lime pies work well with a crumbly graham cracker crust, but after a few tests, we picked a shortcrust pastry for our coconut cream pie. To make sure it's perfect, be sure to blind bake it until golden, as it won't be baked a second time once the cream filling is added.

COCONUT MUST For the star ingredient of this recipe, we recommend the method popular in the United States, which is to combine the sweetened shredded coconut with the filling. For a pretty presentation and to highlight the coconut, we also toast some shredded coconut and sprinkle it on the whipped cream topping.

SMOOTH FILLING The key to a good coconut cream pie is its generous filling. We use cornstarch and flour to thicken the filling, as they provide a smooth texture. The 2 eggs used make for a rich flavor and a lovely yellow color, for a nice visual contrast to the whipped cream topping.

Pecan Pie

PREPARATION 30 minutes
COOKING 55 minutes
COOLING 3 hours
SERVINGS 8
FREEZES WELL

Crust

1¼ cups	(190 g) unbleached all-purpose flour
½ tsp	baking powder
¼ tsp	salt
½ cup	(115 g) cold unsalted butter, diced
⅓ cup	(75 ml) milk

Filling

½ cup	(115 g) unsalted butter
1 cup	(250 ml) corn syrup, preferably golden
½ cup	(105 g) brown sugar
3	eggs
2 tbsp	(30 ml) whiskey (optional)
1 tsp	(5 ml) vanilla
1 pinch	salt
1 tbsp	unbleached all-purpose flour
1½ cups	(150 g) raw pecans (not roasted)

Crust

In a food processor, blend the flour, baking powder and salt. Add the butter and pulse a few times, until it forms pea-sized pieces. Add the milk. Pulse just until the dough starts coming together. Remove the dough from the food processor and shape into a disc with your hands.

On a floured work surface, roll the dough into a circle about ⅛ inch (3 mm) thick. Line a 9-inch (23 cm) glass pie dish with the dough. Remove the excess dough hanging over the edge of the pie dish, leaving a ½-inch (1 cm) border all the way around. Tuck the border of dough under itself to form a thick crust. With your fingers, crimp the dough in a series of curves to make a decorative pattern. Refrigerate.

Filling

With the rack in the lowest position, preheat the oven to 375°F (190°C).

In a deep pot over medium heat, cook the butter until it is starting to brown and stops foaming. Pour into a large glass bowl.

Add the corn syrup and brown sugar to the bowl of brown butter. Whisk to combine. Add the eggs, whiskey, vanilla and salt. Mix well. Stir in the flour.

On a work surface, chop half of the pecans. Add the chopped and whole pecans to the bowl of filling and mix well. Pour the filling into the chilled crust.

Bake for 45 minutes or until the crust is nicely browned and the filling has puffed up. Let cool for 3 hours before serving. The pie will keep for 3 days, covered, in the refrigerator.

UNIQUE BAKING To keep the pie crust from drying out, we chose not to blind bake it for this recipe. Instead, we bake it only once, after the filling is poured into the raw pie dough—given that the dough contains lots of sugar, it becomes very hot and has ample time to cook. And because we added plenty of butter, the crust will be extremely flaky, too.

RAW PECANS There's no need to toast the pecans beforehand, as they'll toast perfectly while baking. We therefore use raw pecans, because otherwise they'll get overly toasted and have a burned and bitter taste.

HALF AND HALF We like a mix of whole and chopped pecans. The irregular shape of the chopped nuts fills pockets in the filling nicely, while the whole nuts rise beautifully to the surface for a striking presentation.

MILD FLAVORS This pie's delicious depth of flavor comes from the brown butter and a splash of whiskey. Corn syrup, a staple of this pie from the American South, gives the filling its smooth texture but tones down the sweetness thanks to its just moderate sweetening power.

Strawberry Shortcake

PREPARATION 45 minutes
COOKING 55 minutes
COOLING 3 hours
MARINATING 15 minutes
SERVINGS 8 to 10

Cake

1 cup	(150 g) unbleached all-purpose flour
1 tsp	baking powder
¼ tsp	salt
3	eggs, separated
1 pinch	cream of tartar
1¼ cups	(265 g) sugar
½ cup	(115 g) unsalted butter, softened
1 tsp	(5 ml) vanilla
½ cup	(125 ml) milk

Vanilla Strawberries

1½ cups	(210 g) fresh strawberries, sliced
1 tbsp	sugar
1	vanilla bean, split lengthwise and seeds scraped

Whipped Cream

1½ cups	(375 ml) 35% whipping cream
3 tbsp	sugar
1 tsp	(5 ml) vanilla
	Fresh strawberries, whole or quartered, for decorating

Cake

With the rack in the middle position, preheat the oven to 350°F (180°C). Butter the sides of an 8-inch (20 cm) springform pan and line the bottom with parchment paper.

In a bowl, combine the flour, baking powder and salt. Set aside.

In another bowl, whisk the egg whites and cream of tartar with an electric mixer until soft peaks form. Gradually whisk in ½ cup (105 g) of the sugar until stiff peaks form. Set aside.

In a third bowl, whisk the remaining sugar, the butter, egg yolks and vanilla with an electric mixer. With the machine running on low speed, add in the dry ingredients alternating with the milk.

Stir one-quarter of the meringue into the batter to thin it out. Using a spatula, gently fold in the remaining meringue. Pour into the prepared pan.

Bake for 55 minutes or until a toothpick inserted in the center of the cake comes out clean. Unmold immediately and let cool completely on a wire rack, about 3 hours.

Vanilla Strawberries

In a bowl, combine the strawberries, sugar, vanilla seeds and pod. Let sit for 15 minutes. Drain. Remove and compost the vanilla pod. Set aside.

Whipped Cream

Meanwhile, in another bowl, whisk the 35% cream, sugar and vanilla with an electric mixer until stiff peaks form. Set aside.

Assembly

Cut the cake in half horizontally to have a total of 2 cake layers.

Spread 1 cup (250 ml) of the whipped cream on the cut-side of each cake layer. Spread the vanilla strawberries over the whipped cream layer on one of the cakes. Cover with the second cake, cream-side down. Transfer the cake to a serving dish. Garnish the top of the cake with the remaining whipped cream. Decorate with the fresh strawberries. The cake will keep for 2 days, covered, in the refrigerator.

VERSATILE BASE We achieve the perfect shortcake texture for this recipe using a classic butter cake base enriched with whipped egg whites for extra lightness. Incorporating the egg whites well before baking ensures an even rise. The result is a cake with good mouthfeel and a buttery taste that will neither harden in the fridge nor have a dry texture when you bite into it, as is usually the case with butter-based cakes. It's also the ideal base for other desserts like Yule log cakes or dessert loaves.

WHIPPED CREAM A firm, lightly sweetened whipped cream works best here, letting the strawberries shine. For a touch of fragrance, we add a few drops of quality vanilla extract.

ESSENTIAL STRAWBERRIES We use two kinds of strawberries: macerated strawberries, flavored with vanilla bean and sugar, which soak into the cake's center, and fresh strawberries for the topping, adding brightness and beautiful visual appeal.

Chocolate Cake

PREPARATION 45 minutes
COOKING 50 minutes
COOLING 3 hours
SERVINGS 8 to 10
FREEZES WELL

Cake

2 cups	(300 g) unbleached all-purpose flour
1 tsp	baking soda
1 tsp	baking powder
½ tsp	salt
2	eggs
2 cups	(420 g) sugar
1 cup	(250 ml) buttermilk (see note)
½ cup	(125 ml) vegetable oil
2 tsp	(10 ml) vanilla
¾ cup	(75 g) cocoa powder
¾ cup	(180 ml) strong coffee, at room temperature

Ganache

16 oz	(450 g) 55% to 65% dark chocolate, chopped
1¾ cups	(430 ml) 35% cream
2 tbsp	(30 ml) clear corn syrup

Cake

With the rack in the middle position, preheat the oven to 350°F (180°C). Butter the sides of two 8-inch (20 cm) springform pans and line the bottoms with parchment paper.

In a bowl, combine the flour, baking soda, baking powder and salt. Set aside.

In another bowl, whisk together the eggs, sugar, buttermilk, oil and vanilla.

In a third bowl, whisk together the cocoa powder and coffee. Pour into the bowl with the egg mixture. Stir in the dry ingredients and mix until smooth. Divide the batter between the prepared pans.

Bake for 45 to 50 minutes or until a toothpick inserted in the center of a cake comes out clean. Let cool completely on a wire rack, about 2 hours, before unmolding.

Ganache

Meanwhile, place the chocolate in a bowl.

In a small pot, bring the 35% cream and corn syrup to a boil. Pour over the chocolate. Let sit for 2 minutes without stirring.

Whisk the ganache until smooth. Refrigerate for 1 hour or until thickened but still spreadable, stirring four or five times. If the ganache is too stiff, melt it in the microwave oven for a few seconds at a time, stirring often.

Assembly

Cut off the rounded tops of the cakes to make them as flat as possible. Cut each cake in half horizontally to have a total of four cake layers.

Divide the ganache among the cake layers, spreading it evenly over the surface with an offset spatula. Stack the four cakes one on top of the other and place on a serving dish. The cake will keep for 3 days, covered, at room temperature.

| NOTE | The buttermilk can be replaced with 1 cup (250 ml) milk mixed with 1 tbsp (15 ml) white vinegar or lemon juice. Let sit for 5 to 10 minutes. Stir before adding to the recipe.

A PINCH OF SALT In many desserts salt is used to enhance the flavor. Here, it heightens the chocolate's intensity, allowing its rich taste to take center stage.

BUTTER OR OIL After multiple tests, we found butter adds flavor but tends to dry out the crumb. Vegetable oil, however, keeps the cake moist and tender for days.

COCOA POWDER Cocoa adds a deeper color and more intense flavor than chocolate. Mixing it with warm coffee enhances its taste and helps break up any lumps, allowing it to blend smoothly into the batter.

GOURMET GANACHE For a rich yet balanced frosting, we recommend a ganache made with chocolate containing 55% to 65% cacao. Anything higher and the ganache may become bitter. Stir until just smooth and silky; overmixing leads to crystallization and a grainy mouthfeel.

Key Lime Pie

PREPARATION 30 minutes
COOKING 45 minutes
CHILLING 4 hours
SERVINGS 8 to 10

Crust

1¼ cups	(175 g) graham cracker crumbs
⅓ cup	(75 g) unsalted butter, melted
1 tbsp	sugar
⅛ tsp	salt

Lime Cream

1 tsp	cornstarch
¾ cup	(180 ml) juice from key limes (about 25) or regular limes (6 to 8) (see note)
¼ cup	(60 ml) sour cream
1 tbsp	lime zest, plus more for serving
3	eggs
1 can	(10 oz/ 300 ml) sweetened condensed milk

Whipped Cream

1 cup	(250 ml) 35% whipping cream
2 tbsp	sugar

Crust

With the rack in the middle position, preheat the oven to 350°F (180°C).

In a bowl, combine the graham cracker crumbs, butter, sugar and salt. Press the crust along the bottom and up the sides of a 9-inch (23 cm) glass pie dish. Bake for 15 minutes. Let cool.

Lime Cream

In a bowl, combine the cornstarch and lime juice until smooth. Add the sour cream, lime zest, eggs and condensed milk and whisk until smooth. Pour into the cooled crust.

Bake for 30 minutes or until the edges of the lime filling are set but the center is still slightly wobbly.

Cover with plastic wrap directly on the surface of the pie. Let cool. Refrigerate for 4 hours or until the filling has completely set and chilled.

Whipped Cream

In a bowl, beat the 35% cream and sugar with an electric mixer until stiff peaks form. Transfer to a pastry bag fitted with a star tip. Garnish the pie with rosettes of whipped cream. Sprinkle with lime zest.

| NOTE | Remove the zest from the limes before juicing them.

UPPER CRUST Getting our pie's foundation just right means butter is key. But how much? We recommend ⅓ cup (75 g), enough for the crust to hold together without becoming heavy and cloying. This makes the graham cracker crumble easier to press into the pie dish and gives it a cookie-like consistency once baked. We also add a smidgen of salt to make the overall flavor pop.

KEY FIGURES We use 6 to 8 regular limes, or about 25 small key limes in this recipe. The latter have a punchier, more acidic profile compared to typical grocery store limes, which are less tangy and more fragrant. The good news? Both versions are delicious! It really depends on your personal preference and which lime variety you can easily find.

GENEROUS FILLINGS Along with lime juice and condensed milk, we add sour cream to the filling. Smooth and tangy, the sour cream enhances the flavor but also introduces extra liquid, which makes the filling sweat during baking. To counter this, we add a touch of cornstarch, which helps solidify the mix and creates a wonderful wobbly texture. We tried using egg yolks only, but found that 3 whole eggs provide the rich, flan-like texture we're aiming for.

GET COOKING Because our filling is quite thick, the best results came from baking it for about 30 minutes, roughly double the classic key lime bake time. The result? A cohesive pie that seamlessly merges crust and lime cream.

Pavlova with Berries and Lemon Curd

PREPARATION 40 minutes
COOKING 2 hours
COOLING 2 hours
SERVINGS 8

Meringues

1½ tsp	cornstarch
1½ tsp	(7.5 ml) lemon juice
3	egg whites, at room temperature
¾ cup	(160 g) sugar

Lemon Curd

¼ cup	(55 g) sugar
3	egg yolks
1	egg
1	lemon, zest finely grated
¼ cup	(60 ml) lemon juice
2 tbsp	butter

Mascarpone Cream

¼ cup	(60 ml) mascarpone cheese
1 tbsp	sugar
½ cup	(125 ml) 35% whipping cream
½ tsp	(2.5 ml) vanilla

Toppings

1 cup	(150 g) fresh blueberries
1 cup	(140 g) fresh strawberries, sliced
1 cup	(135 g) fresh raspberries
	Mint or lemon balm leaves (optional)

Meringues

With the rack in the middle position, preheat the oven to 200°F (95°C). Line a baking sheet with a silicone mat or parchment paper.

In a small bowl, combine the cornstarch and lemon juice until smooth.

In a bowl, whisk the egg whites until frothy. Gradually whisk in the sugar until stiff peaks form. Using a spatula, gently fold in the cornstarch mixture.

Using a ⅓-cup (75 ml) ice cream scoop, spoon eight balls of meringue onto the prepared baking sheet, evenly spaced out. Using a wooden spoon or spatula, make a well at the center of each ball.

Bake for 2 hours or until the meringues are dry and no longer stick to the silicone mat or parchment paper. Turn off the oven and leave the meringues there to dry for 2 hours, keeping the oven door slightly ajar with a wooden spoon.

Lemon Curd

Meanwhile, in a pot off the heat, whisk together the sugar, egg yolks, egg and lemon zest until smooth. Add the lemon juice and butter. Cook over medium heat, stirring constantly and scraping the bottom and sides of the pot, until the mixture thickens and starts to boil. Remove from the heat. Strain through a sieve set over a bowl, pressing down with the back of a ladle. Compost the zest.

Cover with plastic wrap directly on the surface of the curd. Let cool. Refrigerate for 1 hour or until completely chilled.

Mascarpone Cream

In a bowl, whisk the mascarpone and sugar with an electric mixer until smooth and creamy. Add the 35% cream and vanilla. Whisk until soft peaks form.

Toppings

Divide the lemon curd among the meringues. Garnish with the mascarpone cream and berries. Decorate with mint leaves.

MAKING A MERINGUE A traditional pavlova is known for its crunchy meringue shell and airy interior. To create it, we use the simple French method with four ingredients. Adding 3 egg whites gives it plenty of volume. After baking for 2 hours at a low temperature, followed by 2 hours of drying time, the meringue stays crisp on the outside but maintains its bright white color on the surface. This preparation is easy to portion for individual servings.

LEMONY CREAM This version of curd, a creamy lemon spread, is deeply satisfying. Its secrets? The perfect balance between buttery richness and tangy acidity, with a firm yet creamy texture that ensures a perfect hold (no drips). The 3 yolks we set aside from the meringue mean you can make a generous amount of curd.

MASCARPONE VERSION The pavlova is a story of textures, with mascarpone cream adding body and silkiness in every bite. It's our twist on the classic recipe that usually calls for whipped cream.

Carrot Cake

PREPARATION 50 minutes
COOKING 50 minutes
COOLING 3 hours
SERVINGS 10 to 12
FREEZES WELL

Cake

2 cups	(300 g) unbleached all-purpose flour
1 tbsp	baking powder
1½ tsp	ground cinnamon
1 tsp	baking soda
¾ cup	(180 ml) vegetable oil
¾ cup	(160 g) sugar
¾ cup	(160 g) brown sugar
3	eggs
3 cups	(330 g) grated carrots (about 4 large carrots)
1 can	(14 oz/398 ml) crushed pineapple, drained

Cream Cheese Frosting

1 block	(8 oz/250 g) cream cheese, softened
½ cup	(115 g) unsalted butter, softened
1 tsp	(5 ml) vanilla
1 cup	(130 g) icing sugar

Cake

With the rack in the middle position, preheat the oven to 350°F (180°C). Butter the sides of two 8-inch (20 cm) springform pans and line the bottoms with parchment paper.

In a bowl, combine the flour, baking powder, cinnamon and baking soda.

In another bowl, whisk the oil, sugar and brown sugar with an electric mixer. Add the eggs and mix until smooth. Using a wooden spoon, stir in the carrots, pineapple and dry ingredients. Divide the batter between the prepared pans.

Bake for 50 minutes or until a toothpick inserted in the center of a cake comes out clean. Let cool on a wire rack. Unmold and let cool completely, about 3 hours.

Cream Cheese Frosting

In a bowl, cream the cream cheese, butter and vanilla with an electric mixer until smooth. Gradually beat in the icing sugar until the frosting is smooth and creamy.

Assembly

Place one cake on a serving dish. Spread ¾ cup (180 ml) of the frosting over the surface. Top with the second cake. Cover the entire cake with the remaining frosting. The cake will keep for 5 days, covered, in the refrigerator. Let sit out at room temperature before serving.

A GOOD BALANCE When it comes to classic recipes, it's easy to overdo the oil and sugar. In developing this version, we reduced both to create a less caramelized and lighter cake that lets the carrot's natural sweetness shine through. Pineapple adds moisture and another sweet touch, which too much sugar or oil would have masked.

NOSTALGIC PINEAPPLE We use canned pineapple to stay true to the version of this cake we grew up with. We wanted to keep things simple and go back to basics, so chose not to add any nuts or raisins; but if you would like to, ½ cup of each will suffice.

AN IDEAL PAN We bake the cake in two pans to prevent it from being too thick and baking unevenly for too long. In our opinion, 2 layers also offers the best cake-to-frosting ratio. You can also opt for two square pans if you prefer.

COMPACT FROSTING We reduced the sugar in both the batter and the frosting. Too much sugar can make the frosting too firm, so we used only the amount of sugar needed to yield a silky cream cheese texture with just enough sweetness.

Italian Bomboloni Doughnuts

PREPARATION 50 minutes
RISING 2 hours 10 minutes
COOKING 35 minutes
COOLING 2 hours
MAKES 1 dozen

Doughnuts

½ cup	(125 ml) warm water
4 tsp	instant yeast
1 cup	(250 ml) 35% cream
1	clementine or ½ orange, zest finely grated
1	lemon, zest finely grated
1 tsp	(5 ml) vanilla
4½ cups	(675 g) unbleached all-purpose flour
½ cup	(105 g) sugar
1 tsp	salt
4	egg yolks
3	eggs
	Vegetable oil, for frying
	Sugar, for coating

Pastry Cream

1 cup	(210 g) sugar
⅓ cup	(50 g) unbleached all-purpose flour
2 tbsp	cornstarch
6	egg yolks
2	eggs
4 cups	(1 L) milk, warmed
2 tsp	vanilla

Doughnuts

In a bowl, combine the water and yeast. Let rest for 5 minutes.

In another bowl, combine the 35% cream, citrus zest and vanilla.

In a stand mixer fitted with the dough hook or in a large bowl using a wooden spoon, combine the flour, sugar, salt, egg yolks and eggs. Add the yeast and cream mixtures. Mix until the dough comes together.

In the stand mixer or on a floured work surface, vigorously knead the dough for 5 minutes or until smooth. Shape the dough into a ball and place in a clean, lightly floured bowl. Cover with a damp kitchen towel and let rise in a warm, humid spot for 2 hours.

Pastry Cream

Meanwhile, in a pot off the heat, whisk together the sugar, flour and cornstarch. Whisk in the egg yolks, eggs, ½ cup (125 ml) of the milk and the vanilla until smooth. Whisk in the remaining milk. Bring to a boil over medium heat, whisking constantly and scraping the bottom and sides of the pot, just until the mixture thickens. Strain through a sieve set over a bowl to remove any lumps.

Cover with plastic wrap directly on the surface of the pastry cream. Let cool. Refrigerate for 2 hours or until completely chilled.

When ready to use the pastry cream, mix with a spatula until creamy and smooth. Transfer to a pastry bag fitted with a ½-inch (1 cm) star tip.

Frying

Preheat the oil in a deep fryer to 340°F (170°C). Line a baking sheet with paper towels.

Place some sugar in a bowl. Set aside.

On a generously floured work surface, roll the dough into a rectangle about ½ inch (1 cm) thick.

→

Using a 3½-inch (9 cm) round cookie cutter, cut out 12 doughnuts. Set aside on a lightly floured baking sheet. Use any dough scraps. Cover with a damp kitchen towel and let rest for 10 minutes, until the doughnuts have risen slightly.

Carefully drop two doughnuts at a time in the hot oil and cook for 3 to 4 minutes or until nicely browned, turning them over halfway through cooking. Watch out for splattering. Drain on the paper towels. Coat with sugar. Let cool on a wire rack.

Assembly

Using the point of the star tip, pierce a hole in the top center of the cooled doughnuts. Fill with the pastry cream. Serve immediately or refrigerate and enjoy them ideally the same day.

BRIOCHE EFFECT This type of doughnut originating in Italy uses a brioche-style dough filled with pastry cream. Its soft, rich texture comes from plenty of egg yolks, which moisten the dough and help promote its rise.

VERSATILE CREAM For these doughnuts, we used cream instead of butter, to play the role of both fat and liquid. This makes the dough easier to work with and knead while creating softness.

RICH PASTRY CREAM We are generous with egg yolks in the pastry cream here, too. The result is a beautifully yellow, creamy filling, like the ones found in Italy, with a taste reminiscent of crème brûlée.

STUFF 'EM The perfect doughnut should be substantial when you hold it in your hand. That's how you know you've added enough pastry cream, which also keeps each bite tender and moist!

Cheesecake

PREPARATION 25 minutes
COOKING 2 hours
COOLING 7 hours 30 minutes
SERVINGS 10 to 12
FREEZES WELL

Crust

1¼ cups	(175 g) graham cracker crumbs
2 tbsp	sugar
¼ cup	(55 g) unsalted butter, melted

Filling

1¼ cups	(265 g) sugar
2 tbsp	unbleached all-purpose flour
4 blocks	(8 oz/250 g each) cream cheese, softened
¾ cup	(180 ml) sour cream
4	eggs
2	egg yolks
1 tsp	(5 ml) vanilla

Crust

With the rack in the middle position, preheat the oven to 350°F (180°C). Line the bottom of an 8-inch (20 cm) springform pan with parchment paper.

In a bowl, combine the graham cracker crumbs, sugar and butter. Press gently along the bottom of the prepared pan. Bake for 12 minutes. Let cool completely, about 30 minutes. Generously butter around the inside of the pan.

Tightly wrap the base and around the outside of the pan with a double layer of 18-inch-wide (45 cm) heavy-duty foil, letting it extend upward above the rim of the pan. Reduce the oven temperature to 325°F (165°C).

Filling

In a food processor, combine the sugar and flour. Add the cream cheese, sour cream, eggs, egg yolks and vanilla and blend until the mixture is smooth. Using a spatula, scrape down the sides of the food processor as needed. Pour the filling over the cooled crust.

Place the cheesecake in a large baking dish. Fill the baking dish with enough hot water to come halfway up the sides of the springform pan.

Bake for 1 hour 50 minutes or until a thermometer inserted in the center of the cake reads 150°F (65°C). Remove the cake from the water bath. Remove the foil. Let cool for 1 hour. Cover and refrigerate for 6 to 8 hours or until completely chilled. Freeze at this point, if desired.

Run a thin blade between the side of the pan and the cake to unmold. Transfer the cake to a serving dish. The cheesecake will keep for 4 days, covered, in the refrigerator.

TEXTURE AND AROMA We love the incomparable softness of this cake. Sour cream adds tanginess and lightness to the rich cream cheese base, while egg yolks create a creamier texture and warm color. For the aroma, we preferred classic vanilla, though lemon zest makes a respectable alternative. You can even choose to use both!

MIX WELL When preparing the filling, combine the sugar and flour first to break up any lumps. Mix until smooth, being careful not to overmix as this can make the batter frothy and affect the texture. Once smooth, pour the filling into the springform pan.

HOT WATER BATH For best results, bake the cheesecake in a hot water bath. To prevent water from seeping in, wrap the pan tightly with two layers of aluminum foil before placing it in a large baking dish and then pouring boiling water around it. If the top browns too quickly, lay a sheet of foil over the pan without sealing it.

UNMOLDING The cake is done when the edges are set but the center still jiggles slightly. When ready, remove it from the hot water bath, cool and then run a thin blade between the inside of the pan and the cake. Skipping this step can cause cracking as the cake cools and contracts.

Chocolate Éclairs

PREPARATION 1 hour
FREEZING 30 minutes
COOKING 45 minutes
COOLING 3 hours 30 minutes
SERVINGS 6
FREEZES WELL

Craquelin Topping

¼ cup	(40 g) unbleached all-purpose flour
3 tbsp	brown sugar
2 tbsp	unsalted butter, softened

Crème Légère

½ cup	(105 g) sugar
3 tbsp	unbleached all-purpose flour
4 tsp	cornstarch
1	egg
1	egg yolk
1½ cups	(375 ml) milk
1 tsp	(5 ml) vanilla
½ cup	(125 ml) 35% whipping cream

Choux Pastry

¼ cup	(60 ml) water
¼ cup	(60 ml) milk
¼ cup	(55 g) unsalted butter
1 tsp	sugar
1 pinch	salt
½ cup	(75 g) unbleached all-purpose flour
2	eggs

Chocolate Glaze

6 oz	(170 g) 50% to 60% dark chocolate, chopped
1 tbsp	(15 ml) vegetable oil

Craquelin Topping

In a bowl, combine the flour, sugar and butter until smooth. Between two sheets of parchment paper, roll the mixture out until 1⁄8 inch (3 mm) thick. Remove the top sheet of parchment. Using a knife, cut the craquelin into six 5½ × 1¼-inch (14 × 3.5 cm) rectangles. Freeze for 30 minutes or until ready to assemble the éclairs.

Crème Légère

In a small pot off the heat, whisk together the sugar, flour and cornstarch. Add the egg and egg yolk. Mix well. Add the milk and vanilla. Bring to a boil over medium heat, stirring constantly and scraping the bottom and sides of the pot, just until the mixture thickens. Remove from the heat. Strain through a sieve set over a bowl to remove any lumps.

Cover with plastic wrap directly on the surface of the pastry cream. Let cool. Refrigerate for 3 hours or until completely chilled. When ready to use the pastry cream, mix with a spatula until creamy and smooth.

In another bowl, whisk the 35% cream with an electric mixer until stiff peaks form. Using a whisk, fold the whipped cream into the pastry cream. Refrigerate the crème légère until ready to assemble the éclairs.

Choux Pastry

Meanwhile, in a pot, bring the water, milk, butter, sugar and salt to a boil. Remove from the heat. Add the flour all at once and stir vigorously with a wooden spoon until the mixture forms a smooth ball that pulls away from the sides of the pot, about 2 minutes.

Return the pot to medium heat and cook, stirring, for 3 to 4 minutes to dry out the dough. This step is crucial for a successful choux pastry. A thin film will form on the bottom of the pot once the dough has sufficiently dried out. Transfer to a bowl or into the bowl of a stand mixer.

Using a wooden spoon or the paddle attachment, mix the dough for 5 minutes to cool it and draw out the humidity. Add the eggs one at a time, mixing well between each addition, until the mixture is shiny and smooth.

With the rack in the middle position, preheat the oven to 375°F (190°C). Line a baking sheet with a silicone mat or parchment paper.

Transfer the choux pastry into a pastry bag fitted with a ¾-inch (2 cm) plain tip. On the baking sheet, slowly pipe the choux pastry into six logs, each about 5½ inches (14 cm) long and ¾ inch (2 cm) wide, evenly spaced out.

Place the rectangles of craquelin on the logs, being careful not to crush them.

→

Bake for 20 minutes. Reduce the oven temperature to 325°F (165°C). Bake for another 20 minutes or until nicely browned. Let cool completely on a wire rack. Freeze at this point, if desired.

Make a hole in each éclair by running the round handle of a wooden spoon from one end to the other (see note). Using a pastry bag fitted with a ½-inch (1 cm) plain tip, fill the hole of each éclair with the light cream.

Chocolate Glaze

In a glass bowl large enough to dip the éclairs, melt the chocolate in the microwave oven for 1 to 2 minutes, stirring every 30 seconds. Whisk in the oil.

Quickly dip the top of each éclair into the chocolate glaze, tilting the pastry from side to side to get even coverage. Refrigerate for 30 minutes before serving. The éclairs will keep for 3 days in an airtight container in the refrigerator.

| NOTE | Instead of using the handle of a wooden spoon, you can pierce three holes in the bottom of each éclair using a ½-inch (1 cm) pastry tip in order to fill them from underneath.

INCREDIBLE CRAQUELIN Topping the choux pastry with a craquelin adds both irresistible texture and visual appeal. It helps the pastry hold its shape and puff up evenly as it bakes—and it gives a delightful crispness when you bite into it.

CRÈME LÉGÈRE Our filling combines pastry cream and whipped cream for a light, airy texture. It also combines the strengths of two starches: flour for firmness and cornstarch for smoothness, creating a perfect balance. The eggs have two uses here, with the whites giving the cream structure and the yolks making it silky. Vanilla extract brings a nice, even color to the cream.

CHOUX PASTRY For best results, we use an easy-to-handle choux pastry for our éclairs. Don't skip the drying-out stage: cooking the dough in the pot helps evaporate moisture so it puffs evenly in the oven.

CHOCOLATE GLAZE To enhance the éclairs, we chose a light chocolate glaze made with 50% to 60% cacao for a subtle bitterness. A touch of oil gives it a glossy shine, keeps the chocolate from blooming and creates a sauce-like texture rather than a thick ganache.

Apple Pie

PREPARATION 45 minutes
COOKING 50 minutes
CHILLING 1 hour 30 minutes
SERVINGS 8
FREEZES WELL

Filling

¼ cup	(55 g) butter
1 cup	(210 g) sugar
10 cups	(1.1 kg) peeled and cored Cortland apples, each cut into 8 wedges (about 8 to 10 medium apples)
2 cups	(220 g) peeled and cored McIntosh apples, each cut into 8 wedges (about 2 medium apples)
¼ tsp	ground cinnamon

Crust

2 cups	(300 g) unbleached all-purpose flour
¼ tsp	salt
1 cup	(225 g) cold unsalted butter, diced
⅓ cup	(75 ml) ice water
1 tsp	(5 ml) apple cider vinegar or white vinegar
	Milk, for brushing

Filling

In a large non-stick skillet over medium heat, melt the butter. Add the sugar and mix well. Cook for 1 minute. Add all of the apples and the cinnamon. Cook over high heat, stirring, for 10 minutes or until the McIntosh apples are reduced to a purée, the Cortland apples are very soft and the cooking syrup is almost dry. Transfer to a bowl and let cool. Refrigerate for 1 hour 30 minutes or until the filling has completely chilled.

Crust

Meanwhile, in a food processor, blend the flour and salt. Add the butter and pulse a few times, until it forms pea-sized pieces. Add the water and vinegar. Pulse just until the dough starts coming together. Remove the dough from the food processor and shape into two discs with your hands. Cover with plastic wrap and refrigerate for 30 minutes.

Assembly

With the rack in the lowest position, preheat the oven to 425°F (220°C).

On a floured work surface, roll out the two discs of dough until about ⅛ inch (3 mm) thick. Line a 9-inch (23 cm) round, 1-inch (2.5 cm) deep glass pie dish with one disc of dough.

Using a small ½- to ¾-inch (1 to 2 cm) round cookie cutter or a plain pastry tip, cut out 5 circles from the second disc of dough.

Pour the apple filling into the bottom of the dough-lined pie dish, forming it into a mound at the center of the pie.

Brush the edge of the dough with milk. Cover with the second disc of dough and remove any excess dough as needed. Fold the edge of the top disc under the bottom disc. Seal the dough together by pressing on the edge of the pie with your fingers or a fork. Brush the surface of the pie with milk.

Bake for 35 minutes or until the crust is nicely browned. Let cool. Serve with vanilla ice cream, if desired. The pie will keep for 3 days, covered, at room temperature.

FILLING FINDINGS In our view, the best apple pie should taste of, well . . . apples! And to achieve that, it needs as many apples as possible. During testing, we discovered that precooking the apples before filling the dough is a game changer. First, it allows you to fit more apples into the pie (12 instead of the usual 4 to 6). Second, since the apples release most of their water during precooking, there is no excess liquid to soak into the crust. And a note on shape: we recommend apples cut into wedges as they release much less liquid than diced apples while baking.

CHOOSE YOUR APPLES For apple pie, the Cortland variety is ideal for its firm, melt-in-the-mouth texture. But we've always known we also wanted to include some McIntosh because they break down more quickly and compote is excellent to bind all the apples together.

A TOUCH OF ACIDITY When it comes to pastry, a touch of acidity keeps the dough lighter by breaking down the proteins in the flour. We tested several kinds, but in the end, found cider vinegar complements the apples perfectly. Note: white vinegar also yields excellent results.

Tarte Tatin

PREPARATION 50 minutes
COOKING 1 hour 35 minutes
COOLING 1 hour 25 minutes
SERVINGS 8

Flaky Shortcrust Pastry

1½ cups	(225 g) unbleached all-purpose flour
½ tsp	salt
¾ cup	(170 g) cold unsalted butter, thinly sliced
6 tbsp	(90 ml) ice water
1 tbsp	(15 ml) apple cider vinegar

Apples

8 to 9	medium Gala or Cortland apples, peeled, cored and quartered
¾ cup	(160 g) sugar
¼ cup	(60 ml) water
2 tbsp	unsalted butter
1 tbsp	(15 ml) apple cider vinegar
1	vanilla bean, split lengthwise and seeds scraped

Flaky Shortcrust Pastry

In a bowl, combine the flour and salt. Using your fingertips, incorporate the butter into the flour until flaky. Gradually add the water and vinegar, mixing just until the dry ingredients are moistened, making sure to leave pieces of butter intact. Add more water as needed. The dough will be soft and sticky.

On a floured work surface, roll the dough out to form an 11 × 8-inch (28 × 20 cm) rectangle. Using a pastry brush, remove any excess flour. Fold the dough in three widthwise. Fold the dough in half lengthwise to form a square. Cover with plastic wrap. Refrigerate for 45 minutes or until firm. The dough will keep for 2 days in the refrigerator.

Apples

With the rack in the middle position, preheat the oven to 375°F (190°C).

In a 10-inch (25 cm) cast-iron skillet, arrange a circle of apple wedges, rounded-side down, around the outside edge, overlapping them slightly. Continue to arrange the apples in tight concentric circles to cover the entire bottom of the skillet. Set aside.

In a small pot, bring the sugar and water to a boil. Cook, without stirring, until an amber caramel forms. Remove from the heat.

Gradually whisk the butter, vinegar and vanilla seeds into the caramel. Watch out for splattering. Stir until smooth.

Pour the caramel evenly over the apples. Transfer the skillet to the oven and bake for 35 minutes.

Assembly

Meanwhile, on a floured work surface, roll the chilled dough out to form a 12-inch (30 cm) square. Using a 12-inch (30 cm) round plate as a guide, cut out a circle of dough. Refrigerate the circle of dough on the plate while the apples bake.

→

Remove the apples from the oven, being careful not to spill any liquid. Place the circle of dough over the apples, tucking the edge of the dough inside the skillet. Continue to bake for 45 minutes.

Remove the skillet from the oven. Tilt the skillet slightly to verify the quantity of liquid remaining. The liquid should be very thick and syrupy, but not completely evaporated. If there is too much, continue to bake, checking on the quantity of liquid every 5 minutes. Remove the skillet from the oven and let cool for 10 minutes.

Run a thin blade between the side of the skillet and the apples. Flip the tart out onto a serving dish. Be careful; the handle of the skillet will still be hot. Let cool for at least 30 minutes.

Cut the tarte tatin into wedges. Serve with vanilla ice cream or whipped cream, if desired. Although the tart will keep for 2 days in the refrigerator, it is best enjoyed warm the same day it is made. If refrigerated, let sit out at room temperature before serving.

CRUST WITH BITE We've tried puff pastry before to make the sheet of dough needed for this recipe, but it's often too brittle to bite into. Instead, we highly recommend this flaky pastry that's halfway between a puff pastry loaded with butter and a shortcrust pastry, which has more body. Cold butter is essential here for the pastry, as softened butter can blend into it and compromise the formation of the pastry's layers.

FIRM APPLES Apple wedges arranged in a rosette shape are the hallmark of a tarte tatin. For the fruits to keep their shape when cooked and not break down, we suggest Gala or Cortland apples, which yield similar results. Depending on their ripeness, some apples may release more juice than others, so keep an eye on the amount and consistency of the liquid left by the end of the baking time, and continue baking for longer as needed.

THE RIGHT SKILLET The type of skillet you use can affect the results depending on its material. We prefer cast-iron because it retains the heat and distributes it evenly, ensuring even caramelization across the apples. A stainless-steel skillet will also do the job.

GOLDEN CARAMEL The caramel you pour over the apples should have an amber hue. Its exact color and flavor will depend on how you cook the sugar; the longer you cook it and the higher the temperature, the darker and more bitter the caramel becomes. We aim for a golden, perfectly balanced caramel for this tart.

Black Forest Trifle

PREPARATION 1 hour
COOKING 45 minutes
COOLING 15 hours
SERVINGS 12

Pastry Cream

⅓ cup	(70 g) sugar
3 tbsp	unbleached all-purpose flour
2 tbsp	cocoa powder
1 pinch	salt
1	egg
2 cups	(500 ml) milk, warmed

Morello Cherries

6 tbsp	(80 g) sugar
2 tbsp	cornstarch
1 jar	(19 oz/540 ml or 24 oz/680 g) morello cherries in light syrup
2 tbsp	(30 ml) lemon juice
2 tbsp	(30 ml) kirsch

Genoise

½ cup	(75 g) unbleached all-purpose flour
3 tbsp	cocoa powder
¼ tsp	baking powder
¼ tsp	baking soda
3	eggs, at room temperature
½ cup	(105 g) sugar
2 tbsp	(30 ml) vegetable oil

Whipped Cream

2½ cups	(625 ml) 35% cream
3 tbsp	sugar
1 tsp	(5 ml) vanilla

Toppings

	Chocolate shavings
6	fresh cherries (optional)

Pastry Cream

In a small pot off the heat, whisk together the sugar, flour, cocoa powder and salt. Add the egg and mix well. Add the milk. Bring to a boil over medium heat, stirring constantly and scraping the bottom and sides of the pot, just until the mixture thickens. Simmer for 1 minute while stirring. Transfer to a bowl.

Cover with plastic wrap directly on the surface of the pastry cream. Let cool. Refrigerate for 3 hours or until completely chilled. The pastry cream will keep for 2 days in the refrigerator. When ready to use, stir with a whisk until creamy and smooth.

Morello Cherries

Meanwhile, in a pot off the heat, combine the sugar and cornstarch. Add the cherries with their syrup and the lemon juice. Bring to a boil while stirring. Add the kirsch and continue to cook for 30 seconds. Transfer to a bowl.

Cover with plastic wrap directly on the surface of the cherry mixture. Let cool. Refrigerate for 3 hours or until completely chilled.

Genoise

Meanwhile, with the rack in the middle position, preheat the oven to 350°F (180°C). Butter an 8-inch (20 cm) square pan and line with parchment paper, letting it hang over all four sides.

In a bowl, combine the flour, cocoa powder, baking powder and baking soda. In another bowl, whisk the eggs and sugar with an electric mixer until the mixture is pale, tripled in volume and falls from the beaters in a ribbon, about 10 minutes (using a stand mixer is preferable). With the machine running on low speed, drizzle in the oil.

Sift the dry ingredients over the egg mixture and gently fold in using a whisk. Spread the batter out in the prepared pan.

Bake for 30 minutes or until a toothpick inserted in the center of the cake comes out clean. Let sit on a wire rack for 2 hours or until completely cooled.

→

Assembly

Unmold the cake. On a work surface, cut the cake into cubes.

In a bowl, whisk the 35% cream, sugar and vanilla with an electric mixer until stiff peaks form.

In a 12-cup (3 L) glass serving bowl, spread out ¾ cup (180 ml) of the pastry cream. Top with one-third of the cake cubes, one-third of the cherry mixture (about ¾ cup/180 ml) and 1 cup (250 ml) of the whipped cream.

Repeat these steps two more times, finishing off with the remaining cherry mixture. Refrigerate the remaining whipped cream. Cover the bowl of trifle and refrigerate for 12 hours.

Garnish the trifle with the remaining whipped cream, chocolate shavings and fresh cherries.

ADD PASTRY CREAM Traditional Black Forest cake may not contain pastry cream, but it's a must in a trifle. We enhance the chocolate flavor by incorporating cocoa powder into the pastry cream. The genoise, with its subtle chocolate notes, then absorbs the cream beautifully. We also used flour instead of cornstarch to make the pastry cream firmer.

INTENSE CHERRY FLAVOR For this essential Black Forest component, we use sour (morello) cherries to enhance the trifle and give it a more pronounced tartness than sweet cherries provide once cooked. Morello cherries are usually sold in jars in light syrup at most grocery stores; alternatively, canned bing cherries work well too.

WHIPPED GENOISE Genoise typically gets its lift from whipped eggs, but we give it a boost here by adding leavening agents like baking soda and baking powder for extra volume. A touch of oil instead of butter makes the cake even softer.

A HEAD START Each component of this trifle can be prepared ahead of time. We recommend assembling the dessert at least 12 hours, and up to 2 days, ahead of serving. This allows the textures to meld and the cake to soak up the pastry cream and cherry juice. Assembling it too close to serving time will result in slightly bland, less developed flavors.

RICARDO

Thank You to the Best Team

This book was made possible thanks to a wonderful team who truly worked diligently, starting with our test kitchen. A big thank-you goes to Isabelle, Etienne, Danielle, Laurence, Alexane, Nicolas, Lisa and Kareen who, over the years, have developed the recipes, tested them almost a dozen times each and standardized them.

As for our content team, they managed to make everything beautiful and inviting through their words and images. Thanks to Maude, our content and creative director, for her excellent ideas; writer Charline-Ève, who managed to take the test kitchen's technical information and make it clear and simple, along with our translators, Vicki and Michelle; our art director, Geneviève, for her inspiration and care with the page layout, along with our graphic designers Ève and Etienne; and our graphic artists Karine and Pascale, for their vision.

Given that we first eat with our eyes, photos and images are clearly very important. Thank you to our photographers, Jean-Michel, Christian, Maude, David, Sophie, Dana and Mathieu; our accessories stylists, Sylvain, Caroline Nault and Caroline Simon; and food stylists, Etienne, Nicolas, Anne and Nataly. You all played a part in making this book beautiful.

For this book to be a success from start to finish, we needed solid and foolproof organization. Thanks to our project managers, Martine and Gaelle, who conducted everything like an orchestra, along with our studio director, Josée, who optimized each and every step in the creation of this book. And I don't want to forget Nathalie, Audrey-Anne, Alexandre and Marika, the team who makes you want to flip through this tome through their promotional skills.

I want to give a special thanks to Lindsay and Robert at Appetite, Penguin Random House Canada, who once again put their trust in us.

Thanks to Brigitte, my partner in work and life, who joins me at every taste testing. She has a critical sense and an intuition that always leads us toward making the best decisions.

And finally, I want to thank you, our dear readers, for making this book possible. It's your comments and observations that helped us to adapt, modify and refine our recipes until they were better than best.

Ricardo

Index

APPETIZERS AND SIDES

Buffalo Chicken Wings, 37
Fried Calamari, 30
Fried Onion Rings, 35
Fully Loaded Baked Potatoes, 29
Homemade Fries, 15
Mashed Potatoes, 43
Ratatouille, 113
Scalloped Potatoes, 45
Vermicelli Rice, 132

SAUCES AND DIPS

Béarnaise Sauce, 121
Bolognese Sauce, 81
Homemade Chunky Ketchup, 21
Hummus, 33
Spaghetti Sauce, 93
Tartar Sauce, 140
Tzatziki, 27

SOUPS AND SALADS

Caesar Salad, 16
Clam Chowder, 115
French Onion Soup, 38
Gazpacho, 19
Minestrone Soup, 41
Pea Soup, 22
Wonton Soup, 24

BREAKFASTS

Baked Beans, 71
Blueberry Muffins, 65
Chocolate-Hazelnut Spread, 62
Crusty White Bread, 61
Eggs Benedict, 67
French Omelet, 54
Leek and Ham Quiche, 68
Pancakes, 50
Raspberry Scones, 57
Salmon Gravlax, 73
Scrambled Eggs, 53
Thin Breakfast Crepes, 49
Ultra-Moist Banana Bread, 59

MAIN DISHES

BEEF

Beef Bourguignon, 123
Beef Tartare, 109
Chili con Carne, 144
Prime Rib Roast with Béarnaise Sauce, 121
Steak au Poivre, 106

CHICKEN

Barbecue Chicken Skewers, 147
Butter Chicken, 139
Chicken Pot Pie, 98
Chicken Shish Taouk, 132
Coq au Vin, 118
Fried Chicken, 126
Hunter's Chicken Stew, 117
Oven-Roasted Barbecue Chicken, 94
Portuguese-Style Grilled Chicken, 131
Souvlaki Skewers, 135

EGGS AND CHEESE

Leek and Ham Quiche, 68
Swiss Cheese Fondue, 124

FISH AND SEAFOOD

Clam Chowder, 115

Coquilles St. Jacques, 101

Crab Cakes, 140

Paella, 149

Salmon Pot Pie, 102

Salmon Tartare, 110

LAMB

Moussaka, 136

PASTAS AND PIZZAS

Meat Lasagna, 78

Margherita Pizza, 89

Mushroom Pizza, 90

Pasta Carbonara, 82

Pizza Dough, 87

PORK

Barbecue Ribs, 143

Maple-Braised Ham, 97

Souvlaki Skewers, 135

RICE

Mushroom Risotto, 85

Paëlla, 149

TURKEY

Roasted Whole Turkey with Stuffing, 153

Stuffed Turkey Roast, 150

VEAL

Meatballs in Tomato Sauce, 77

Veal Blanquette, 105

VEGETARIAN

General Tao Tofu, 129

Ratatouille, 113

Swiss Cheese Fondue, 124

DESSERTS

Apple Crisp, 172

Apple Pie, 208

Black Forest Trifle, 215

Carrot Cake, 197

Cheesecake, 203

Chewy Chocolate Chip Cookies, 159

Chocolate Cake, 190

Chocolate Éclairs, 205

Chocolate-Hazelnut Brownies, 170

Coconut Cream Pie, 184

Date Squares, 167

Italian Bomboloni Doughnuts, 199

Key Lime Pie, 193

Lemon Poppy Seed Loaf, 169

Maple Pudding Cake (Pouding Chômeur), 163

Maple Syrup Pie, 178

Oatmeal Cookies, 160

Pavlova with Berries and Lemon Curd, 194

Pecan Pie, 187

Slow Cooker Chocolate Pudding Cake, 175

Strawberry Shortcake, 188

Tarte Tatin, 211

Tiramisu, 177

Vanilla Cake, 181

Vanilla Frosting, 183

Vanilla Ice Cream, 165